Tucholsky Wagner Zola Scott Sydow Freud Schlegel
Turgenev Wallace Fonatne Twain Walther von der Vogelweide Fouqué Friedrich II. von Preußen
Weber Freiligrath Kant Ernst Frey
Fechner Fichte Weiße Rose von Fallersleben Richthofen Frommel
Engels Fielding Hölderlin
Fehrs Faber Flaubert Eichendorff Tacitus Dumas
Feuerbach Maximilian I. von Habsburg Fock Eliasberg Zweig Ebner Eschenbach
Ewald Eliot Vergil
Goethe Elisabeth von Österreich London
Mendelssohn Balzac Shakespeare Dostojewski Ganghofer
Trackl Stevenson Lichtenberg Rathenau Doyle Gjellerup
Mommsen Tolstoi Hambruch Droste-Hülshoff
Thoma Lenz Hanrieder
Dach Verne von Arnim Hägele Hauff Humboldt
Karrillon Reuter Rousseau Hagen Hauptmann Gautier
Garschin Defoe Baudelaire
Damaschke Descartes Hebbel
Hegel Kussmaul Herder
Wolfram von Eschenbach Dickens Schopenhauer Rilke George
Bronner Darwin Melville Grimm Jerome
Campe Horváth Aristoteles Bebel Proust
Bismarck Vigny Voltaire Federer Herodot
Gengenbach Barlach Heine
Storm Casanova Tersteegen Grillparzer Georgy
Chamberlain Lessing Langbein Gilm Gryphius
Brentano Lafontaine
Strachwitz Claudius Schiller Kralik Iffland Sokrates
Katharina II. von Rußland Bellamy Schilling
Gerstäcker Raabe Gibbon Tschechow
Löns Hesse Hoffmann Gogol Wilde Vulpius
Luther Heym Hofmannsthal Gleim
Roth Klee Hölty Morgenstern Goedicke
Heyse Klopstock Kleist
Luxemburg Puschkin Homer Mörike
Machiavelli La Roche Horaz Musil
Navarra Aurel Musset Kierkegaard Kraft Kraus
Nestroy Marie de France Lamprecht Kind Kirchhoff Hugo Moltke
Nietzsche Nansen Laotse Ipsen Liebknecht
Marx Ringelnatz
von Ossietzky Lassalle Gorki Klett Leibniz
May vom Stein Lawrence Irving
Petalozzi Knigge
Platon Pückler Michelangelo Kafka
Sachs Poe Kock Korolenko
de Sade Praetorius Mistral Liebermann Zetkin

The publishing house tredition has created the series **TREDITION CLASSICS**. It contains classical literature works from over two thousand years. Most of these titles have been out of print and off the bookstore shelves for decades.

The book series is intended to preserve the cultural legacy and to promote the timeless works of classical literature. As a reader of a **TREDITION CLASSICS** book, the reader supports the mission to save many of the amazing works of world literature from oblivion.

The symbol of **TREDITION CLASSICS** is Johannes Gutenberg (1400 – 1468), the inventor of movable type printing.

With the series, tredition intends to make thousands of international literature classics available in printed format again – worldwide.

All books are available at book retailers worldwide in paperback and in hardcover. For more information please visit: www.tredition.com

tredition was established in 2006 by Sandra Latusseck and Soenke Schulz. Based in Hamburg, Germany, tredition offers publishing solutions to authors and publishing houses, combined with worldwide distribution of printed and digital book content. tredition is uniquely positioned to enable authors and publishing houses to create books on their own terms and without conventional manufacturing risks.

For more information please visit: www.tredition.com

# Three years in France with the Guns: Being Episodes in the life of a Field Battery

C. A. Rose

# Imprint

This book is part of the TREDITION CLASSICS series.

Author: C. A. Rose
Cover design: toepferschumann, Berlin (Germany)

Publisher: tredition GmbH, Hamburg (Germany)
ISBN: 978-3-8495-0639-1

www.tredition.com
www.tredition.de

# Three Years in France with the Guns.

C. A. ROSE, M.C.

# INTRODUCTION.

These brief notes of experiences with the guns for thirty-eight months in France were primarily penned for my own satisfaction. Friends who read the manuscript expressed much interest in it, and added the hope that it might be given a more permanent form. Hence it is that it is now printed for private circulation.

The story is a simple record of the fortunes of my own Battery and Brigade, and is intended as a tribute to the good comradeship which existed, under all conditions, among all ranks.
C.A.R.
Edinburgh,
*January, 1919.*

# CONTENTS.

The "Grey Battery" at St. Omer, May 1917

# CHAPTER I. (p. 001)

### Breaking Us In.

On a morning early in August, 1915, the Brigade disembarked at Havre without mishap to man, horse, or material, and proceeded to a Rest Camp on the outskirts of the town. We were in France at last! The same evening the Batteries started to entrain, and every two hours a complete unit was despatched up the line to an unknown destination. The men received refreshments at various Haltes, and the horses were duly watered and fed, but the journey was, on the whole, long and tedious. On one occasion only was the monotony broken, and that unwittingly, by the humour of one of the officers. In the course of the evening, the train stopped at a small station, and the compartment in which the officers were settled drew up in front of the Buffet. Some one asked where we were, and a subaltern, anxious to display his newly-acquired knowledge of French, replied, "Bouvette," which called forth no response. Shortly afterwards the train proceeded on its way, and the occupants of the carriage settled themselves down to sleep. All passed quietly for the next couple of hours — then the train stopped once more, and, as luck would have it, again our carriage came to a standstill directly opposite the buffet of the station. At once a question was asked as to our whereabouts. The same subaltern, shaking himself out of a deep slumber, stretched, roused himself, and, peering out of the window, exclaimed, "Good Lor', still at this beastly hole, 'Bouvette'!" He expressed much surprise at the "unseemly mirth," as he described it, which followed!!

After detraining, the Battery marched through beautiful country, which reminded one of the Borders, as it was not unlike the valley of the Tweed, and we were at once taken to the hearts (p. 002) of the inhabitants of the good village of Seningham, which place was destined to be our home for the next few days. The officers were afforded spacious accommodation in the house of the Maire, whilst the men had comfortable billets in the neighbourhood. Time was spent making our unit shipshape after its travels by land and sea, and the "hairies" obtained as much grazing as possible, to make them fit for what was in store for them. It was wonderful how quickly the men adapted themselves to French ways, and much amusement was caused by their eager, if somewhat unsuccessful, attempts to master the language of our Allies.

When it became known that the officers were anxious to increase their knowledge of the language of the country, the maidens of the village vied with one another to obtain posts as instructresses, and there was nearly a free fight amongst them for the possession of our worthy Senior Subaltern, whose taking ways did not fail to catch their attention!

But, alas! our peaceful warfare was not to be for long! One morning sudden orders came through to prepare for the line in a couple of days' time. All was instant bustle, extra grooming was given to the horses, and finishing touches were put to the howitzers and vehicles. We were to be given a trial in action to show how we would comport ourselves before joining the "Feet" of our own Division, the Guards, who at that time were out at rest. For this purpose we were to be placed under the orders of the C.R.A. of an Indian Division, to reinforce the Batteries already in positions and receive instruction from them.

At last the morning arrived to move off, the column, skirting the town of St. Omer, took the main road to Hazebrouck, and, as we passed through the village of Arques, we caught a first glimpse of our future infantry. They appeared equally keen on seeing their new artillery, and inspected us with a critical eye. The march was made in easy stages, and on the morning of the third day the Brigade arrived at Merville, a quaint old town in Flemish Flanders. After a hasty lunch, the officers rode ahead, in order to get into touch with the unit we were to support in the line, and another amusing incident happened *en route*. One of the Junior Officers owned a sturdy mare, whose reputation as a charger was apt to be ridiculed by his companions, as she was notorious for her slow gait. When the party had proceeded some distance at the trot, "Halting Hilda" was observed, to the astonishment (p. 003) of everyone, to be gradually taking the lead. This fact called forth the remark from her master, "By Jove, she is pulling extraordinarily hard to day: what can be the matter with the animal?" It was then discovered that the rider had been at her mercy for the last couple of miles, the bit clanking merrily from side to side under her great jaw. In the hurry and excitement of departure, after lunch! the bit had not been replaced in her mouth!

The afternoon was spent in reconnoitering the gun positions allotted to us, which were the alternative positions of the units already in line. As a rule, each battery makes a second or alternative gun position, in case it should be shelled out of its existing one, so that no delay takes place in getting into action again. When night fell there was subdued excitement in the wagon line as the time drew near to take the guns "in." This was actually the beginning of our first venture — would we have the luck to get there without being caught in the enemy's harassing fire? How would we behave under shell-fire: would we be steady or otherwise? All these and many other questions flashed through our minds, for a great deal depends, more than one would believe, on how a new and inexperienced unit receives its baptism of fire.

At length a start was made, and the Battery moved off, and soon turned down the long, straight main road leading to La Bassée, the trees on either side showing signs of shrapnel scars, and even in the darkness it could be seen that the cottages were, for the most part, in ruins. It felt distinctly eerie as the small column proceeded silently on its way without showing lights of any description; the stillness and darkness broken now and again by the barking of a gun as we drew nearer the battery zone, and by an occasional Verey Light, which seemed to reveal us in all our nakedness. That long stretch of road seemed interminable—were we never going to reach our destination? However, all remained quiet throughout our progress, and at last we arrived at the entrance to the gun position, which was to be our home for the next fortnight. The guns were speedily unlimbered and man-handled into the pits awaiting their reception, the ammunition was unloaded from the vehicles, and the teams were returned to the wagon line.

The following morning the pieces were "layed out" on our particular zone, and we had time to look round and take stock of (p. 004) our new abode, which was a farmhouse standing in the centre of an orchard adjoining the main road. The building itself was by no means intact, although, as yet, habitable. It gave us enough shelter of a kind, and we soon adjusted ourselves to the prevailing conditions, and the outhouses surrounding it afforded ample accommodation for the detachments. The gun pits were cunningly concealed in the front portion of the orchard, special care having been taken against the prying eyes of hostile aeroplanes. We were fortunate in the choice of position made for our first time in the line, for two reasons, firstly, it was an interesting zone—including the village of Neuve Chapelle now immediately behind our front line—and, secondly, it was quiet. The country there is extremely flat, with the exception of Aubers Ridge, which, occupied by the enemy, overlooked us to a certain extent, although the many trees and woods prevented his having an uninterrupted view. Our tuition began at once, and we were conducted to the front line through innumerable communication trenches, which, at first, reminded one of a maze at an exhibition, the only difference being that numerous noticeboards directed our movements.

There we were welcomed, with smiling faces, by men of a Ghurka battalion, their white teeth and flashing eyes showing up their brown skins. Now and then they would stop sharpening their deadly-looking kukris, their dearest possession, to allow us to pass along the trench. Nothing delighted these brave little men more than to be

permitted to go on a silent raid at night, when they wormed themselves through the wire in "No Man's Land," and did as much damage on the other side as possible. They have been known to enter
the enemy trenches without a sound, killing everyone within reach,
and to return radiant, quite unscathed. When questioned as to why
they had not brought in any prisoners for identification purposes,
they would merely roll their eyes, shrug their shoulders, and say,
"Enemy all quiet, he asleep," and calmly remove the still warm gore
from their knives! Continuing on our way, we next struck a High-
land regiment, the necessary complement of the one of stout little
men just left behind. It was most interesting, as one had heard so
much about the traditional good comradeship existing, in India,
between Ghurka and Highlander, and here they were still side by
side in France. Their mutual admiration is boundless and uncon-
cealed, and (p. 005) it was most amusing to watch the little men
aping the ways of the big Highlanders, who look huge in compari-
son with them. The Ghurka regiments have their own pipe bands,
and play them as if they, too, had been born and bred in the moun-
tains and glens of Scotland.

Soon we came to a fire bay, specially well placed to obtain a good
view of the enemy trenches, which had been converted into what is
known as an O.P., *i.e.*, an artillery observation post. These O.P.'s are
manned during daylight by the F.O.O. (Forward Observation Officer) and his signaller assistants. Their job is to keep a close watch
on hostile trenches, watching for any unusual movement or for the
appearance of new constructive works, such as machine gun emplacements or new saps. The O.P. has numerous wires leading into
it, and these come from all the batteries in immediate support of
that part of the line, which are jointly responsible for its defence.
Our own signallers had been out early, and a wire had already been
carefully laid and labelled from our gun position to the O.P., so we
were now ready to register our howitzers on some definite object
behind the enemy lines. A house, or some such landmark which is
shewn on our trench maps, is usually chosen to calibrate upon.
There is little trouble in effecting this, but, at first, there is some
difficulty in following the rounds as they fall, through a periscope,
owing to its small field of vision. It was, however, imperative to
make use of that instrument, in this case, as an enemy sniper,

watchful and on the alert, had already seen the top of it, and from time to time a bullet passed overhead unpleasantly close. This served to remind us to be discreet and to run no risks by exposing ourselves in the slightest degree above the parapet. Sometimes it is very difficult to restrain one's enthusiasm when there is an interesting shoot taking place.

The pieces being duly registered, the Battery is now ready for any emergency, and theoretically we can engage any target in our arc of fire. It is then essential to learn the country in hostile territory, and one looks out for likely targets and for points at which one can inconvenience the enemy by keeping him under constant harassing fire. This work must necessarily be done from a point of vantage where a good wide view can be obtained, and, in most cases, a house, tree, or high piece of ground well behind the lines, is selected for a Rear O.P.

In (p. 006) an incredibly short space of time every officer learns the country off by heart, and can bring any gun to bear on a particular target at short notice. At first Junior Officers are allowed practice shoots on targets well behind the enemy lines, and as they gain confidence and experience, are entrusted with "close shoots," *i.e.,* firing on hostile emplacements, etc., in the front line, a job which requires extreme caution and accuracy, as "No Man's Land" averages not more than 200 yards in width in most places. Batteries can always communicate with Battalion Headquarters in the line, a wire, usually buried, leading from there to our Brigade Headquarters, and each Battery has its own private wire to the latter place. In the same way one can be linked up with nearly every unit in a Division by means of an Exchange run by the Royal Engineers.

A few days sufficed us to make ourselves quite at home, and officers went freely about "seeking whom they might devour," visited old established O.P.'s, and searched for new or better ones. It is a curious fact that the average subaltern is never fully satisfied with an O.P., and is always bent on discovering "something better," although in few cases is his ambition realised! One officer favours this O.P., another that, and on this occasion the one which our worthy Battery Commander had a preference for was a most unpleasant place, commonly known as "The Doll's House," though why so called no one could tell. At any rate, it was an abode to be avoided on all possible occasions, and the subalterns were quite convinced it was the registering place of all the hostile batteries within range and vision. At any rate, we daily found less and less of the building, until one day the staircase was blown away as well as the perch on top which afforded us our view. Great was the relief when the B.C. at last declared the O.P. "out of action" until further notice.

Nearly every O.P. has an appropriate name given to it, and so we repaired to "Stink Farm" after abandoning our old love! We put in most useful days of practice there, and the knowledge and experience gained was invaluable. Our thanks were due to the enemy for his consideration in allowing us to conduct our daily tasks almost unmolested: he showed himself to be most lethargic and sleepy, and did not waken up unless we were unusually energetic. Perhaps his chief reason for remaining so inactive was the absence of any heavy guns on our side. Our largest (p. 007) piece was a 60 pdr., and he may have thought mere Field Artillery beneath his consideration. Nor was he more active in the air; his planes rarely passed over our lines, and when they did, it was at so great a height that it was quite impossible for them to gather information. However, one day, we were extremely fortunate in seeing a hostile plane, that had ventured to cross over our lines at a lower altitude, brought down in flames by a direct hit from an "Archie" battery lying in wait close behind our own position. It is a rare sight, for, to tell the truth, anti-aircraft batteries are not held in particularly high respect by anyone except by those of their own ilk, and on only two other occasions did we ever see the like again.

Our fortnight soon sped by, and we were quite reluctant when the time came to go "out." We left our neighbours, who had befriended us so well, with the sincere hope that we would have the good fortune to meet and lie alongside of them again in the future. This hope, however, was not destined to be fulfilled. We retraced our steps through Merville and Aire to the same area from whence we came, to a village called Nielles, in order to concentrate as a Division, which, when formed, was designated the Guards Division.

The inhabitants, as usual, extended a warm welcome to us and showed us every consideration, and we settled down to enjoy the peaceful surroundings bathed in the warm and pleasant September sunshine, while the Senior Subaltern availed himself of the opportunity of again laying siege to the hearts of his former conquests at Seningham close by. Our own C.R.A. came to visit us here, and the officers were severally introduced to him. He expressed satisfaction at the report which came to him from the line, concerning our conduct in action, and added that the high opinion formed of us at home had in no wise been diminished, and that our reputation merited the distinction conferred on us of being selected as the Artillery of the Guards from among the many units of the new Army.

Thus we waited, confident in the belief that, whatever we were in the future called upon to do, we would at least put up a good show, and determined to be a credit to the Division of which we now formed a part. We had not long to wait, whispers passed round that we would be up and doing at no distant date, and these rumours proved to be well founded.

## Our First Battle.

Our marching orders came within the next few days. Each unit was provided with portable bridges, which were carried under the wagon bodies, and this, and several other preparations, gave us a good indication that we were out for business. A couple of days trekking brought us to the village of Nedonchel, which proved to be another place of happy memory to our Senior Subaltern. Here we were given a rough idea of the part we were to play in the coming proceedings. Two army corps were to attack, on a six mile front, in the neighbourhood of Loos and, if the assault was successful, the corps in reserve, which included our Division, was to go through and exploit the victory to its fullest advantage. We were to take no part in the initial attack.

Large masses of troops were being moved up behind the battle area, and, in order to screen our movements from hostile aircraft, the latter stages of the journey were to be made under cover of darkness, so the whole of the next day was spent in resting. At nightfall a diversion was caused by a Cavalry Division passing through the village on its way up, and a splendid sight it presented, as one famous regiment followed swiftly on another. It was now almost time for us to make a start, and the good lady of the house had remained out of bed to brew us hot coffee and see us off the premises. As we were about to depart she told us that her old mother, aged 88, who was in the next room, had expressed the desire to see us for a moment, and so we were conducted to the old lady's bedside. She was lying telling her beads, but sat up as we approached and beckoned to each officer in turn, who advanced, knelt, and received a blessing. The inhabitants knew well that a big battle was (p. 009) to be fought quite soon, as the little village had been the scene of great activity during the past few days and, although it was a considerable distance from the line, the preliminary bombardment could be distinctly heard. The low muffled rumble was incessant, and, to-night, seemed, if anything, more intense. Shortly after midnight we set off and disappeared into the darkness, followed by words of good cheer from the villagers and shouts of "Bon chance, messieurs, bon chance."

Passing through Bruay we arrived a few miles behind the battle front on the morning of the assault, which was delivered at an early hour, and soon the news came back that, so far, everything was going well; the village of Loos had already fallen into our hands. As the day wore on, however, and the expected orders to advance were not forthcoming, we suspected that all was not as it should be and our fears were confirmed soon afterwards by instructions being given to prepare to bivouac overnight on the ground close by. What actually happened was this:—The initial attack was successful in capturing and overrunning the enemy's front line trenches over the whole area, but, on advancing to the second trench system a great deal of wire was found to have been left unbroken or untouched by our artillery, and this held the infantry up at vital places. The attack, however, was pressed with great courage and determination, and in some places the flood of men swept on, but, unfortunately, in others, little or no progress was made. The line, consequently, soon presented a crooked, irregular shape, which made the situation difficult and obscure. The enemy, moreover, had anticipated the attack and had large reinforcements at hand which were at once thrown in, and after a ding-dong struggle throughout the day the advance came to an abrupt standstill. Two Divisions from the Reserve Corps were then sent in, and, on the following afternoon, the Guards attacked and helped to a large extent in straightening out a considerable portion of the line. It was not until nightfall of the third day that we entered the battle and took up a position immediately north of Vermelles Station in the back garden of a tow of damaged villas. On our way "in," a couple of cavalry regiments, which had been holding Loos for the last two days and which had just been relieved, passed us. There passed also the remnant of one of the Scottish Divisions which had fought so valiantly and paid so heavy a price. Footsore, weary, and caked with mud from top to toe, with every sign of what they had been through (p. 010) upon them, and heavily laden with "souvenirs" in addition to their full kit, the men could scarcely crawl along. However, just as one battalion came abreast of us, in such condition, the pipes tuned up and at once every head was erect and not a man was out of step as they swung past us; such is the moral force of the bagpipes. It was one of those moments in which a lump rises in the throat and a thrill runs down the spine.

In our new position we speedily learnt what we could do and what we could not do. For instance, the signallers were able to introduce electric light into our abode by tapping a live wire which ran outside, from one fosse to the next, for we were now in the Lens coal district with mines dotted about here and there. On the other hand, we soon learnt to refrain from sleeping or showing lights in the second storey of our billet which was evidently under direct observation by the enemy, who did not take long to acquaint us with the fact.

There was always a good deal of firing to be done each day, for, although the battle may be said to have finished after four or five days, there were several side-shows before the line was adjusted to our liking, and the enemy's fire was almost continuous. This bothered the F.O.O. parties considerably, and communication was difficult to maintain for more than a short time between the front line and Battery. The wire was frequently broken in numerous places, and this kept signallers and linesmen working at high pressure to repair the damage. The O.P.'s were moderately good, with the exception of one in "Gun Trench," where our men held a portion, then came a sand bagged wall occupied on the other side by our opponents which they were able to enter by a **T**-shaped communication trench, then another sand-bagged wall with our infantry beyond. Neither side could shell this trench for fear of injury to their own party, but this did not prevent a lively exchange of bombs, intermingled with various forms and sizes of "Minnies," which were hurled at frequent intervals. Sniping was also rampant, and periscopes, no matter how small, survived not longer than a few minutes. It was from this delightful spot that one of the subalterns arrived at the Battery one evening with his head swathed in bandages like a Sultan's turban. He had been trying conclusions with a "Minnie," and, as this was in the days before the introduction of the steel helmet, the latter had easily come out on top. When the wound was ascertained to be nothing like as serious as the size of the bandage (p. 011) seemed to indicate, he was removed to the wagon line amid jeers from his brother officers, and a few days' rest sufficed to bring him back to duty again.

Now, in one portion of the zone which we were covering, "No Man's Land" extended some 1500 yards in depth, and midway, lying in the valley, were what appeared to be two derelict enemy guns partially camouflaged This aroused the curiosity of the Staff, who called for volunteers to go out and make an investigation and report as to the condition of the sights, etc. Our B.C. gallantly offered his services, in spite of the fact that he was over six feet in height, and presented a most conspicuous figure, and would not be deterred. He set off crawling through the long grass on his perilous journey, and there was a huge grin on his face when he returned. After his report went in we ascertained that the two pieces were nothing more than cleverly constructed dummies formed from cart wheels, telegraph poles and trunks of trees, but it was not until he almost came up to them that he made the discovery.

The detachments meanwhile had settled down, making improvements to their billets and strengthening the gun pits, and were already proving themselves seasoned warriors. On one occasion a nasty accident happened, due to the explosion of a howitzer, caused, as was afterwards proved, by a faulty shell. The complete gun crew, with the exception of the No. 1 in charge, was wounded. Three of their number were temporarily buried by the earth thrown up by the explosion, and it was probably due to that fact that no one was killed. The pit naturally fell to bits and the debris was indescribable, but the Sergeant managed to disentangle himself, and, standing stiffly to attention, reported to the officer on duty, "No. 2 gun out of action, sir!" No time was lost in digging out the injured men, and it was only found necessary to evacuate three of the number to the nearest dressing station — the remainder flatly refusing to go. The layer, in particular, deserved great credit for his grit, for, in spite of having been buried, and having scarcely a hair left on his head and devoid of eyebrows, not to mention the shock to his nervous system, he was again serving his gun 24 hours later, on the arrival of the new piece. Some idea of the force of the explosion can be gathered from the fact that the barrel was found, in two pieces, some 150 yards away, having been blown over a railway (p. 012) embankment, while the breech block, which weighs about a cwt., was discovered, after a 12 hours' search, embedded in the ground six feet below the pit. At this period a considerable number of "prematures" were taking place, and, on one occasion, we ascribed this wounding of two gunners to this cause, but afterwards found out our mistake. An S.O.S. went up after dark, and, at the time of firing No. 3 gun, the layer and another gunner were both badly hit by what appeared to be a "premature" just outside the bore of the piece. Throughout this period we were firing nothing but high explosive shells. Great therefore was our surprise when, three weeks later, letters arrived from both men, who were in hospital, to say that in each case shrapnel bullets had been extracted from them! What had actually occurred was this: At the same time that the trigger was pulled and the shell discharged, a "pip squeak" must have burst in front of the mouth of the gun pit, driving the bullets through the entrance.

Day after day passed in much the same way, neither side attempting to make an attack on any large scale, but on the morning of the 8th October, it was observed that the hostile shelling was not normal, and had increased in extent along the whole recently captured area. Preparations were therefore rapidly made to meet any eventuality, and, as the day advanced and his bombardment gained in strength, it was apparent to everyone that the enemy contemplated an attack. At noon orders were received to be ready, at any time, to lay down a destructive barrage on a certain zone. The Staff had happily anticipated the point of attack accurately, and, by the time the enemy concentrated his final burst of fire on his objectives, every gun in the neighbourhood which could bear, was trained on the vital spot ready to open out. When at last the time arrived, the bombardment ceased abruptly, and the enemy's infantry advanced to the assault wave upon wave, for the most part in mass formation and with arms linked together. Emerging from a wood, they had a considerable distance to cover across open ground before approaching our trenches, so both our infantry and artillery fire was at first withheld. This gave encouragement to the enemy, and, as his bombardment had been pretty severe, he expected more or less of a "walk over," and did not reckon on what was to follow. When (p. 013) he had advanced to within 200 yards of our lines, suddenly rapid fire spurted out from our rifles and machine guns, and guns of every description spat H.E. and shrapnel, and his ranks were literally mown down. Then a curtain was put down behind—a solid wall of fire—which made it practically impossible for the troops to retire, and their plight was beyond all hope. While they were cogitating whether to come on or go back, they were slaughtered in heaps—raked by the deadly machine guns. Very few indeed survived to tell the tale, but one prisoner claimed to be most indignant with the whole proceedings, and expressed his opinion that we did not "play the game" by withholding our fire, and that they imagined they had only to walk into our trenches and take possession of them. This proved to be the last big hostile counter-attack attempted, and indeed both sides were content to remain in their own trenches. We made a smaller attack the next week, but it was also unsuccessful, and little or no ground was gained. The enemy artillery devoted themselves principally to counter battery work, and several British batteries, which were ill concealed, had a most unpleasant time. Free use was made of lachrymatory shell, our first taste of it. One clear, moonlight night the battery was firing at a slow rate, and apparently the enemy saw our flashes, for he speedily turned a 4.2 battery on to us, his shells landing just short of each gun pit. No casualties resulted, but a shell entered the window of one detachment's billet and exploded, completely wrecking the room and destroying the men's equipment. Soon afterwards instructions were issued to change positions, and this was effected without loss or mishap. The new position was more favourably placed, some little way in front of the Fosse at Annequin, and had been constructed by the French. We were now covering the Hohenzollern Redoubt of evil memory. Another O.P. was constructed on the railway embankment on the La Bassée-Vermelles line, which lent itself favourably to the construction of a shaft for protection, the soil, for the most part, being chalk, as indeed it was in all the surrounding neighbourhood. It was our misfortune at this position to say farewell to our Battery Commander, who left us to take up a Staff appointment with the Mediterranean Expeditionary Force, and all ranks were sorry to lose a leader who had thus far shared all their joys and sorrows. At the same (p. 014) time we were fortunate in securing in his successor one who quickly and tactfully took up the reins of office, and the Battery continued to run on equally smooth lines.

It now became quite evident that operations would not resume the nature of a battle, and it was no surprise to receive intimation that the Division would shortly retire from the conflict. Nobody was sorry at the prospect of going out, although useful lessons had been learnt and considerable experience had undoubtedly been gained.

The weather was beginning to break, and towards the end of the first week in November we withdrew to the village of Sailly, preparatory to marching into the nest area for which we were bound.

# CHAPTER III. (p. 015)

## "Peace Warfare."

When it became known that our destination was to be the sector immediately adjoining the one we had already been in, facing Aubers Ridge, our delight knew no bounds, for all were well aware that that locality was considered a "cushy" spot which augured well for the coming winter.

No delay was made in leaving Sailly, and, proceeding by way of Bethune and St. Venant, we arrived at a small hamlet midway between the latter town and Merville. The Battery remained in rest for a few days, while a couple of "subs." with a working party commenced construction on the new position selected by the B.C. This entailed a considerable amount of labour, for timber and all other material had to be carted from the R.E. dump at La Gorgue some distance away. With an eye to comfort as well as concealment, it was decided to dig the pits in an orchard, along some old assembly trenches which had been used by troops before the battle of Neuve Chapelle. Close by was a cluster of cottages and outhouses in a wonderful state of preservation.

By the end of the week the guns were pulled in, although there still remained a lot to do on the position. The house in which the officers quartered themselves was intact, with the exception of a few slates on the roof and several broken window panes. Moreover, there was a little furniture left and there were some fine open fireplaces, so we had every reason to be satisfied. Within a short space of time the gun pits were completed and camouflaged in keeping with the nature of the ground, and great assistance was rendered us during this undertaking by an airman who flew over the position from time to time and pointed out the various deficiencies. At last when he reported that the position could (p. 016) not be seen from a height of 2000 feet we concluded, rightly, that nothing was to be feared in that direction. Thus we settled down to a period commonly known as "Peace Warfare." This may be summed up us a time when one experiences the maximum amount of pleasure that is possible under war conditions, with the minimum amount of discomfort. The enemy were completely deceived as to our whereabouts, and took us to be in another vacant position some way down the road, which was liberally shelled by them whenever fire was opened by us, and we used to encourage this procedure by occasionally ceasing in order to lead him into the belief that he was doing us damage. At all events, the position was never shelled the whole time we were in possession of it—a somewhat unique experience for a battery in France.

The infantry were also kept busy at the commencement of this period, as we had relieved another Indian Division, and on this sector the parapet had been built for the most part by Ghurkas, who, however stout fellows they may be at heart, have not the stature of Guardsmen. The result was the latter found their heads and shoulders showing well above the parapet, and this necessitated the immediate heightening of the same some two to three feet.

The O.P. duties were divided equally between the subalterns, each doing a third daily. The wagon lines were situated east of La Gorgue within easy reach, and frequent visits were paid to them, although no officer remained there permanently.

During our stay here the Battery came under the direct orders of the C.R.A. and was attached to no group in particular. Various tasks were alloted to us, and these were, as a rule, most interesting and instructive. To further increase our knowledge the B.C. gave the majority of these shoots to the Junior Officers, briefly explaining the orders and then leaving us to our own devices by departing for the rest of the day to the wagon lines on the pretext that he had a birthday to celebrate. He had many of them. This plan was much to our liking, and tremendous keenness was displayed by all. Great pains were taken to carry out everything to the letter, and the signallers also carried out their part with equal spirit. The gun detachments at this time rose to a high pitch of proficiency and could get 10 rounds a minute out of the howitzers, which, considering the double load and triple movement, was by no means a bad performance.

A (p. 017) fine level field ran alongside of the position, and it was speedily made use of as a recreation ground. Goal posts were erected, and often a hot contest at football would be interrupted by the shrill blast of a whistle summoning the men hastily to action. Their task completed, they would calmly return and finish the game.

All kinds of mutual understandings existed between the opposing sides in this area, which we soon learnt and respected. For instance, the village of Aubers lay behind the enemy lines approximately at the same distance that Laventie did on our side. Both were used as Brigade Headquarters and filled with troops. Neither town was shelled unless the enemy accidentally dropped a shell into it, when instant retaliation was forthcoming. On one occasion the placid calm of Laventie was rudely shaken through the instrumentality of a young officer in one of our sister brigades who, unconscious of what he was doing, planted several shells into Aubers. The consequence was the following conversation took place over the telephone between Headquarters and the offending subaltern.

"Hullo! Is that Ack Battery?"

"Yes, sir. Just a moment, sir. I'll put you through to the mess, sir."

"Right you are, but look sharp about it, please. Yes. Hullo! Is that an officer? Well, I say, have you been firing just now?"

"Yes, sir. So-and-so is doing a practice shoot from the O.P."

"Put me on to him at once."

"Yes, sir."

A brief interval follows, in which various mutterings are overheard by the signaller in the exchange, who smiles to himself as he continues to listen.

"Hullo! hullo!! Damn these young officers! Will they never learn to answer quickly? Slow, slow is not the word for it. Will have to go round and shake them up a bit. This is absurd. Hullo! there. Hullo! Is he never going to come? Exchange, can't you get him?"

"Just a moment, sir."

"Hullo! hullo!!"

"Yes, sir. So-and-so speaking."

"What the devil are you firing at, young sir?"

"Well, sir, I was given permission to fire a few rounds— —"

"Where?" (p. 018)

"At the cross roads, sir."

"Seen any of them fall?"

"Not as yet, sir."

"Well, for God's sake stop firing at once, sir. Why, man, your shells are dropping in Aubers, and they are retaliating like the very devil. There goes another, just outside."

"Very sorry, sir. Couldn't make out where the shells were falling."

"Well, report to me as soon as you get back, remember. Have no time to listen to an explanation now."

"Very good, sir. Good-bye, sir."

An animated discussion now takes place in the telephone exchange, and the unanimous opinion is that poor So-and-so is "for it" and will perhaps even get the sack, and who will succeed to the Right Section if he leaves the Battery?

In these days a walk along the front line was a delight, and nothing gave the F.O.O. greater pleasure than to take his morning constitutional from one end of our area to the other and to peer over the side at frequent intervals by means of a periscope. Sniping was sometimes indulged in, but a target rarely presented itself for the simple reason that the enemy was hardly ever in his front line trenches during daylight. From one O.P. we could often see one or two men running along the trenches with lighted torches kindling fires and causing smoke in order to lead us into the belief that the trenches were powerfully manned.

Now, about this time, a number of hostile batteries, whose positions could not be located, gave us a certain amount of trouble, but a successful ruse was carried out which enabled us to discover them. Operations were undertaken in order to force the enemy to show his hand, and every indication was made by us that we were about to institute a raid. Wire cutting was done by one battery, and others registered strong points in rear behind the prescribed area. Then at dusk, known as flesh time, when batteries are most likely to give their positions away, all the O.P.'s were manned, spotting apparatus made ready, and our barrage was put down on this sector. The infantry had been provided with dummy figures, which they held aloft on poles, and in the semi-darkness this gave the impression that they were preparing to quit the trenches and go over the top, while high overhead hovered a number of our aeroplanes waiting to assist. The plan worked (p. 019) admirably, and in a few minutes the enemy's counter preparation commenced. As the result of our efforts his positions were pin-pointed and dealt with by our 60-pdrs. the next day, after which we were not bothered by them to such a great extent.

Soon after this episode there came upon the scene what were commonly known as "Cook's Tourists." These were officers whose units were still at home, and who were sent out to gain experience by being attached to batteries for a short period. At times the tourist laid himself open to being the victim of many practical jokes, and this certainly contributed to the liveliness of the mess. A certain officer was escorted down to the front line trenches one day, and, as usual, the party was armed with periscopes. All of a sudden he emitted a cry of delight, as, gazing through the instrument, he told us of how crowds of the enemy were walking along a road. Could we not get our guns on to them quickly? This seemed an incredible occurrence, as, in this sector, not a single German had been seen for days on end. The mystery was speedily solved, however. By some means or other, he had been holding the periscope so that it faced the opposite direction, and what he actually saw was a party of our own men walking leisurely along the road some way behind our lines. Needless to say, this officer came in for a considerable amount of chaff, and, in course of time, was solemnly presented with a paper medal, suitably inscribed, on which reversed periscopes figured prominently.

The festive season was now drawing near, which necessitated the gathering of provisions, for the men were to celebrate the 25th of December by having a special dinner, and presently leave was opened to our unit and the first lucky ones departed for "Blighty." Some sort of gift was due the enemy on this occasion, and it took the shape of a sharp five minutes' bombardment, from every gun in the area, on the stroke of midnight on Xmas Eve. In spite of this gruelling, the enemy next morning showed signs of wishing to fraternise with our men in the front line, but strict orders had been issued in advance that this was not to be countenanced. The Germans showed themselves freely above the parapet, and one could see that they had been dressed up smartly for the occasion, probably in order to impress us with their appearance. However, there was "nothing doing." Little or no sniping took place, but the artillery went through their usual routine, in fact rather increased their fire that (p. 020) day. The men's dinner was a great success, and all seemed pleased with their fare—pork and potatoes, vegetables, plum pudding and fruit, with plenty of beer or stout to wash it down. The Officers' Mess was lively also, and our first 'Xmas, under war conditions, was voted most successful. Next day the Padre turned up, and a service was held in one of the barns, but, in the middle of the address, on "Peace on earth, goodwill towards men," there was a sudden call for "action." A rush was made to the guns, and, after a few minutes' argument with the enemy, we returned and finished listening to the discourse. Somehow or other one could not help feeling that the two happenings were incongruous!

We had a notion that perhaps the enemy would make an attempt to retaliate on us at New Year for our little joke on 'Xmas Eve, and this proved to be correct. He made rather a feeble demonstration, and it was speedily squashed, as we were awaiting it. It was an extraordinary thing, but we always found our foe very slow in the uptake: it generally took him quite a week to think out some measure of retaliation, and when it came, it consisted, as a rule, in copying what we had done to him. We could usually count on that and consequently guard against it.

One day instructions came through calling for a report on a new charge, for reducing the flashes when night firing, which was supposed to be in our possession. Our worthy Senior Subaltern was at that time in command, so he decided to have the trial the same evening and put in his report at once. The remaining officers were to "stand by" at the guns and first fire a salvo with the ordinary charge and then one with the new one, while he stood some distance in front to wait the results. All went well and the salvoes were duly fired, although, at the battery end, there did not appear to be any difference between them, which fact was unanimously agreed upon. However, that was not the opinion of the Senior Subaltern, who waxed eloquent on the "soft, velvety colour" of the new charge. This was all set down presently, in a lengthy dispatch covering, at least, two columns of "foolscap," and sent to the Brigade. Nothing further was heard for several days, then a telephone message came through which brought a smile to the face of everyone in the mess except the officer concerned. It ran as follows: — "Reference my B214 of (p. 021) the 9th inst. Report on flash reducing charges is herewith cancelled. The production of same has not yet been issued to batteries in the field A.A.A." Both salvoes had been of the same nature!

Our Right Section Commander had a mania for spy hunting, and it was true that spies were known to infest the neighbourhood and had sometimes actually been caught. On every available occasion this officer would set out to scour the countryside in quest of a suspect. One day this led to the waste of much energy on his part. Having followed hard on the scent of a suspicious character, from one end of our area to the other, the quarry suddenly doubled back along the La Bassée road and disappeared into a house. Our friend entered also, and found himself in a Brigade Headquarters, confronted by the "spy," who greeted him warmly, and asked him what service he could render him, at the same time calling for tea. He had shadowed none other than the chief Intelligence Officer of the Division the whole afternoon! There was nothing for it but to own up and apologise as best he could, to the vast amusement of the Staff Officer. After this incident, we were spared further wild-goose chases by this enthusiast, and the keenness hitherto shown by him for these quests somewhat abated.

A good deal of excitement was caused, at this time, by the arrival of some heavy artillery in our neighbourhood, so much talk had come to our ears concerning them. The guns were duly placed in position, and on the afternoon on which they were to open fire a large turn out of F.O.O.'s collected in the O.P.'s to watch the enemy get a surprise. They did considerable damage, but, at the same time, were largely responsible for stirring up a veritable wasp's nest of hostile heavies which had been lying dormant for ages, and consequently our front again became active.

While our F.O.O. was proceeding one day from the O.P. to the front line, he was caught in one of those bursts of hate and separated from the telephonists who accompanied him. On the conclusion of the shoot, a search was made for him, but he was nowhere to be found. They returned to the Battery and reported the circumstance to the B.C., who, much concerned, speedily organised a search-party, and set out for the scene of action. After a couple of hours weary tramping, they came upon a Company Headquarters in the front line, and there, comfortably ensconced (p. 022) in an easy-chair, with a large whisky-and-soda by his side and a cigarette in his mouth, sat the missing officer. Much indignation was expressed and explanations followed, but, in future, it was only in the last extremity that search parties were instituted!

Thus the days sped by, until it came to the minds of those in authority that the Division had vegetated quite long enough in this area, and, at the beginning of February, we were pulled out and transferred to another sphere of activity.

Everyone regretted leaving this peaceful spot, and the period we spent there was always looked back upon as the brightest and happiest time of our sojourn in France.

# CHAPTER IV. (p. 023)

## In "The Salient."

It soon became known that we were bound for Ypres. This town will, without doubt, be the Mecca in France of the British soldier for all time. This place, above all others, was always mentioned with a voice of reverence and awe, and is hallowed by the presence of the gallant dead who helped in its defence. It was truly the most ill-favoured sector on the whole of the front held by our armies.

Proceeding by way of Hazebrouck and Cassel, we entered the area immediately behind the Salient and took up our quarters near the village of Arneke, for we were not yet due for our spell of duty in the line. At this time the weather was most unpropitious, and rendered training in any shape or form out of the question. The ground was covered with snow to the depth of several inches, and the roads were, for the most part, frost-bound. A Divisional Artillery Horse Show was organised, however, and great keenness was displayed by all the batteries, who spent most of their time horse coping until the day of the event, which was held at Zeggers Capelle. Our Right Section Commander, with a team of fine little blacks, managed to secure the second prize in the principal event.

Several days afterwards we relieved the Division who were holding the left centre of the Salient, and took up our position on the northern extremity of Ypres itself, close to the Dead End of the Canal, a short distance from "Salvation Corner." Here a short description of the position is imperative, in order to give some idea of the awkward nature of this sector and of the conditions attaching thereto. The distance between the jaws of the Salient was some five miles across—from the banks of the Yser Canal at Boesinghe on the north to the neighbourhood of St. Eloi on the south, while the ground held by us extended about two and-a half miles east of Ypres in a semi-circle. Nearly everywhere (p. 024) the enemy was established on rising ground and overlooked our territory, and, with few exceptions, all that was visible to us was his first line system. The enemy was thus enabled to detect any movement behind our line, while we were more or less "blind."

Owing to the confined space through which an entrance into the Salient could be effected, great difficulty was experienced in the matter of transport, as there was only one main artery, namely, the Ypres-Poperinghe road. Every evening at dusk this thoroughfare was crowded with all manner of vehicles, an endless stream, coming and going throughout the night, and from Vlamertinghe onwards the road was subjected to constant shelling, and was enfiladed from either side. Piles of wreckage were always to be seen on the following morning, which told the tale of the previous night's work, and this long, straight piece of road holds more sentiment for the British soldier than any other.

It was soon quite evident that the enemy was acquainted with our location, and it was imperative to prepare an alternative position. A site was chosen across the road, in the garden of a private villa, well sheltered by shrubs and trees. As soon as the work was completed and a communication trench constructed, covered with turf and plants, we commenced moving the guns. This was done without interference from the enemy until the last gun was in the act of being placed in position, when, as luck would have it, a shrapnel shell burst in front of the party, mortally wounding one layer and injuring another. Our B.C., also, who was assisting, received a bullet through his arm, and was forced to leave us. This was the second mishap we had suffered during the course of the first few days, as the Right Section Commander had already been lost to us. Having an insatiable thirst for knowledge, this Officer had left the O.P. with his telephonist in order to explore the front line, which, as everyone who knows the Salient will readily own, was somewhat difficult to recognise in places, especially by a newcomer. Suffering as he did from acute absent-mindedness, it was not surprising that this zealous officer awakened suddenly from his day-dreams to discover that something was wrong, and found himself standing with his companion waist high in a shallow disused trench, which, on further investigation, appeared uncommonly like "No Man's Land!" After a brief consultation, they decided to retrace their steps. Alas! all too late: a hostile sniper, reserving his fire in the (p. 025) hope that they would continue to walk into the enemy trenches, on seeing them turn about, and thus being baulked of his prize and the prospect of a fortnight's leave in his own country, fired a bullet which passed through the thighs of both men one after the other. A party of our infantry, unable to attract their attention and put them right in time, had witnessed this little drama, and proceeded, at great personal risk and at the expense of at least one of their number being wounded, to extricate the two unfortunates and convey them to the nearest dressing station. It was not until a late hour that night that word came to us at the Mess that the missing party had been passed through the prison at Ypres, on their way to a C.C.S. Now, our Battery Commander, after great trouble, had lately gained possession of an improved type of periscope, which he had been persuaded to lend the F.O.O. on that day, and, on receipt of this news, his first thought was for the safety of his precious instrument. The fact that two valuable casualties had resulted did not seem to weigh with him in the least compared with its loss, and he was not to be consoled until it was ascertained that the periscope was in safe keeping. Only then could he be persuaded to make enquiries as to the nature of their wounds and express his sorrow at their misfortune.

The Infantry found the trenches in an appalling state, and forthwith proceeded to repair them, but the enemy would not allow this to go on long, and, after a few days' work had been spent on them, a couple of hours' bombardment would suffice to demolish anything that had been done. As it was a case of labour lost, all attempts at building on a large scale were soon abandoned.

Many interesting excursions were made in and around the town. There was a certain amount of splendour about the ruined place. The high battered remains of the Cloth Hall Tower stood up in proud defiance in the centre of the stricken city, while the ancient ramparts surrounding it gloried in their battle scars and showed a dauntless front to the enemy.

A good deal of annoyance was caused in getting about from place to place through the uncongenial presence of a couple of hostile high velocity guns which were commonly known as "Quick Dick" and "Silent Sue," his consort. They were so named on account of the rapidity with which the shells arrived, and there was little or no warning of their coming. Their chief object (p. 026) was to harass the neighbourhood, for they appeared to have no definite target but just dropped a shell here and there, trapping the unwary and doing considerable damage, as well as effectively raising a certain amount of "wind"!

As conditions suited the enemy admirably, many raids were made by him, and, on one occasion, he launched four simultaneously, one on each sector of the Salient, after a sharp and heavy bombardment. He attacked us between Wieltje and Potijge, but was unsuccessful in his endeavour to obtain an identification. The attempt was frustrated, and the only result was that he left a number of prisoners in our hands.

About the middle of May, the Division came out and returned to the area behind Poperinghe. There was an unexpected treat in store for the Brigade, for it was shortly sent down to the coast for a change of air. A two days' march brought the Battery to Cap Gris Nez, while the other batteries were distributed along the small villages between Calais and Boulogne. It was a real holiday for us, and a better part of the year could not have been chosen. All that was expected of us was to exercise the "hairies," which we did by taking the guns a walk along the hard sand in the early mornings.

A large field was secured, and for several hours daily the horses were put out to grass, and, if ever animals showed signs of joy, they certainly did, and their antics were most amusing to witness. It was expected that some difficulty would be experienced in catching them again, but, after the first day, a trumpet call was all that was required. On hearing the sound, they would throw up their heads, and then slowly wander towards the entrance, where the drivers awaited and secured them.

The main feature of the day was, undoubtedly, the bathing parade, enjoyed equally by man and beast. The horses knew at once what was in store for them when they were led down to the beach. The men stripped, and, mounting the eager horses, a wild dash was made for the water, and quite a number of the animals proved themselves excellent swimmers, many remaining a considerable time in deep water. On leaving the sea, they would gallop along the sands, showing every sign of contentment, and we were glad that, at last, they were receiving some reward for their patient devotion and faithful service, for we were all fond of our four-legged comrades.

Amusements (p. 027) were instituted for the men—all manner of sports by day and concerts in the evenings. The officers lived out of doors, attracted by the cliffs, from which Dover was visible on most clear days, and everyone voted this peaceful place the next best thing to home leave.

It was, therefore, with much regret that, at the end of twelve days, we retraced our steps to Arneke, where we were to remain for the latter portion of the rest.

We had no sooner arrived at this place than the enemy started making himself unpleasant in the southern portion of the Salient, and, attacking the Canadians from Hooge as far as St. Eloi, succeeded in driving them back some distance before he was finally held up. It was quite imperative to retake the ground lost, as he had captured important points of observation overlooking the Salient. A counter attack was set on foot, and we were suddenly called upon to help in the preliminary bombardment and cover the assaulting troops, which included a Brigade of Guards. Just before setting off, our B.C. rejoined us once more, and at two hours' notice we made a beeline for the scene of our future activity. At dusk we entered the ruins of Ypres, and, without delay, proceeded to dig ourselves "in," behind a convent, not far from the south side of the Cloth Hall.

Owing to the number of extra batteries assembled for the operations, we found ourselves without a billet until the genial Commander of a Pioneer Battalion, affectionately known to the entire Dominion Forces as "Big Jim," and credited with innumerable deeds of "daring do," took pity upon us, and invited us to share his hearth and home. This offer we gratefully accepted, and accommodation was also provided for the detachment, and all were made most comfortable.

The bombardment continued for three days, and it became clear, from the enemy's counter preparations, that he was not going to give up his newly acquired gains without a struggle. A most stubborn resistance was offered, and the infantry were forced to fight hard for every foot of ground that was eventually recovered. The bombardment grew in intensity as the zero hour approached. Shortly after midnight, the men went over, and, by breakfast time, had gained all that was required of them, except at one or two points, which were taken without much trouble later.

By the time affairs had settled down normally again, the Division was due in the line, so the Battery pulled out for one night, (p. 028) before transferring to our new zone, which was in the most northerly sector, adjoining the one in which we had already been, and which had an even worse reputation for unpleasantness.

After crossing the Yser Canal, the ground gradually rises towards Pilkem Ridge, and the enemy was ensconced thereon in a kind of stronghold known as the High Command Redoubt. Our trenches lay beneath them, which gave us the feeling of being in a cup encircled round the brim by our foes. During this particular tour, the Battery was split up for the purpose of forming two forward sections, and the greater part of the firing was done by the left section, whose position was well inside the Salient. Its chief object was to harass a certain portion of a hostile trench which was taken in enfilade by it! In order to accomplish this successfully, the guns were placed in an old disused position in a field, near La Brique, on the backward slope of a hill, and the low gun-pits were completely covered with tufts of growing grass. The centre pits were occupied by the two pieces and the outside ones were speedily converted into habitations for the men.

When the trenches were not being subjected to hostile shelling, the enemy devoted most of his time in endeavouring to destroy the numerous O.P.'s dotted about here and there. These were constructed for the most part of reinforced concrete, but the particular one used by us, called "Frascatis," had not yet been discovered, so we were free to carry out shoots to our heart's content.

A favourite diversion was sniping with one of our pieces, which was a particularly accurate one, and several points of observation and snipers' posts were carefully registered. Then we would lie in wait, observe some movement, and let fly one round only. This method exasperated and annoyed the enemy exceedingly.

One of the enemy's principal forms of amusement was to blow parts of our front parapet away and train a machine gun on the space left vacant, and snipe at any unsuspecting person who happened to pass along. On many occasions we were able to bring assistance to the harassed infantrymen, by spotting the offending snipers, and by, in turn, sniping at them with our "How." till we finally silenced them.

At dusk the enemy invariably harassed all roads of communication, and dropped innumerable shells of large calibre into the stricken (p. 029) city; and we made a habit of sitting at the entrance to the little shack, used as the officers' mess, smoking our evening pipes, interested spectators, while the shells screamed overhead, and alighted somewhere in the town, sending up columns of brick dust.

All the batteries in the line were now busy constructing new battery positions, while fresh O.P.'s were also erected, and it was thought that these preparations were preparatory to making an attack to enable us to improve our position by the capture of Pilkem Ridge, but, although the work was completed, nothing further developed.

Soon there were whispers of an impending gigantic attack away down in the south, and for several days before the opening of it our shelling was considerably increased, while the infantry made a series of raids. This was done throughout the whole length of the front, in order to keep the enemy from guessing the exact point of eruption, and we had a warm time in consequence. For a long time after the battle had commenced, we continued making demonstrations, which undoubtedly helped to prevent the removal of many reserves from the locality.

But we were not content to remain here. There was a great scrap taking place elsewhere, and were we going to be left completely out of it, to eat our heads off, in Flanders? It seemed very unlikely that the Division would not be called upon on such an occasion, and great was the joy when one day orders came through that we were soon to proceed to the scene of action. Within two days we pulled out to our old resting place, where preparations were completed for our transference to the battle area.

Our first acquaintance with the dreaded Salient was at an end, and, although the time spent there was always strenuous and difficult, we were not what could be called uncomfortable, and our casualties happily did not exceed expectations.

# CHAPTER V. (p. 030)

**On the Somme.**

At the beginning of August, the Division detrained in the neighbourhood of Doullens, and, proceeding in a southeasterly direction, the Brigade established itself near the small village of Couin. In a few days' time we went "in," and the Battery took up a position on the southern outskirts of Hebuterne, overlooking the enemy stronghold at Serre. This portion of the front was now in a normal state once more, as, on the opening day of the great battle, the British assault from Hamel, northward to Gommecourt, had met with no success, and the attack was not further pressed. The enemy was content to remain quiet, and most of the firing was carried out by us. A considerable number of hostile "Minnies" made conditions somewhat unpleasant for the infantry in the trenches, and during the night the battery position was subjected to indirect machine-gun fire, which necessitated a certain amount of caution in moving about. The O.P.'s were well placed, and afforded us an excellent view, for we overlooked the enemy's lines, and could see some distance beyond them. We were now on the fringe of the battle, and away half right, on clear days, we could see the struggle progressing, as a considerable dent had already been made. The sight was a very grand one, especially after dark. The Verey Lights and various S.O.S. rockets, which were frequently sent up by our opponents, made a fine spectacular display, far finer than any firework exhibition we had ever witnessed in our own country in pre-war days.

Gradually the Division was side-slipped to the south, and our next position was close to the station of Mailly. We did not remain there long, however, as the time had now arrived for us to put in an appearance in the battle itself. We spent one night close (p. 031) to Amiens, and availed ourselves of the opportunity to hold a dinner there, which was attended by all the original officers in the Brigade—a last night of fun and merriment before the long, stiff fight ahead of us, for who knew how many would survive the ordeal. The next day brought us to Vaux, on the River Somme, and, in the first week in September, we found ourselves immersed in the battle. We took up our first position in the lately captured second line

German system, facing Montauban and covering Guillemont, which had just been taken by an Irish Division.

Very stiff lighting was in progress on this sector, as we were now nearing the summit of the Ridge, the possession of which would be invaluable, as the enemy's territory would be laid bare to us, and he would lose his observation over us. It was not surprising, therefore, that he fought with the courage of despair and initiated counter-attack upon counter-attack, all of which we had to meet with great determination. The weather was extremely hot, which added much to the discomfort: and, as progress had been very slow for some time, it was impossible to clear up the battlefield, and the stench was almost insupportable. At length the village of Guinchy was captured, and, with our men installed on the further side of the slope, the fighting for position came to an end. We were now entering on the third stage of the great battle, which had commenced more than two months previously. An attack, on a large scale, was planned, the object being to drive the enemy down the slope of the hill into the low-lying country beyond. Field batteries were moved up into forward positions, in order to assist the infantry, by placing a creeping barrage—a new and most successful invention, after-wards employed on all occasions—in front of the advancing waves of men: and the "heavies," of which, for the first time, we possessed a preponderance, pounded the enemy communications far behind his lines.

The assault was delivered over a wide area, early in the morning of the 15th of September, but in no way did it come up to expecta-tions—in fact, it might almost be counted a reverse. Some divisions did well, and took their objectives, but others were completely held up, at certain strong points, which necessitated the withdrawal of the remainder, in order to keep the line uniform. The Guards met with instant success, and took their final objectives, only to discover that the Division on each side of (p. 032) them had made little pro-gress and could get no further. They were reluctantly forced to re-turn, and it was while doing so that heavy casualties were inflicted on them, as they were raked with fire from the sides as well as in front. During the withdrawal, a party of machine-gunners occupied a trench, and attempted to screen the retirement of the main body of troops, by holding the enemy at bay. In order to use this machine-gun to the best advantage, the piece was placed on top of the parapet, exposed to the full view of the oncoming hordes, but our men never wavered in serving it, and, as soon as one gunner dropped at his post, another instantly took the vacant place, although it meant certain death within a few moments.

Next day they were pulled out to refit, and, as they marched back to rest, a very touching sight was witnessed. A certain battalion, a mere remnant, swung along, headed by its band. All the officers had become casualties, and the Battalion Sergeant-Major was in command, but as many of the dead officers as could be recovered were brought back on stretchers and placed each in his proper position. Headed by the body of their late Commander, the column proceeded on its way, the men marching at attention, and, although covered with mud and blood-stained, they might have been proceeding down the Mall. Such is the discipline of the Guards, and every tribute of respect was paid them by the troops through whom they passed.

The next battle was timed for the 25th inst., and our infantry came back to the line a couple of days before that date. There was much suppressed excitement and curiosity, for the mysterious Tanks were to participate on this occasion for the first time, and it was thought that the secret had been so well kept that they would come as a complete surprise to the enemy. This proved to be the case, and the attack was a great success. What was known as the Flers line was everywhere penetrated, and all gains were held. The Tanks did splendid work. They advanced well ahead of the infantry, and battered down barbed wire, overran trenches, smashed machine-gun emplacements, killing the gun crews, and even waddled as far as the village of Gueudecourt. There they effected much execution and caused great panic among the enemy reserves, which were concentrating for the inevitable counter attack.

Thus the battle continued, sometimes breaking out into fierce fights and at other times reduced to isolated scraps, but all the (p. 033) time the enemy was being gradually and relentlessly pushed down into the valley, and the villages of Morval, Les Boeufs, and Gueudecourt fell into our hands.

It was almost uncanny the way in which villages would completely disappear. For instance, at the time when these hamlets first came within our vision, on our reaching the crest of the hill, they appeared almost intact, but a few days rendered them unrecognisable—they had become merely so many heaps of rubble. There are many places on the Somme which have literally not one brick standing on top of another, and one would never imagine for a moment that a prosperous little village had ever existed there.

Many changes of battery positions were made, and, whenever possible, we burrowed down into the ground, as the enemy's heavy pieces were out after our blood. The great concentration of guns and the few suitable localities for placing them in action added to our difficulties, and we were thus rendered an easy target for the hostile counter batteries. Innumerable brigades were huddled close together, in what was known as the Death Valley, for the simple reason that there was no other suitable spot wherein to place them, and heavy casualties resulted. We had the good fortune, however, to be somewhat isolated from the others, and occupied a forward position, where the guns were hidden in an old German communication trench. The enemy never found it, but subjected us, now and again, to a general burst of harassing fire: his main volume of hate passed us by far overhead.

And, meanwhile, what of our friend the F.O.O.? In those days his lot was by no means an enviable one, and it was a task of no mean magnitude to keep communications going between the trenches and the guns. However, it had to be done, or at least attempted, and the following is a brief account of a typical day in the life of a gunner subaltern.

Orders would be given that a certain hostile trench was to be subjected to a severe, annihilating bombardment, and this necessitated the laying out of a wire to a part of our front line, from which the shoot could be registered, as the target could not be observed from any other locality than the trench immediately opposite it. The F.O.O. rises early in the morning, and sets out with his little squad of telephonists and linesmen. He requires to post a signalman and linesman at frequent intervals, called Relay (p. 034) Stations, in order to preserve communication, as the wire is being continually broken by hostile gun-fire. Progress, in a case like this, is necessarily slow, and he has to pick his way among the shell-holes, seeking as much protection, for the line, as circumstances will permit. The signallers follow in his footsteps, staggering along under the weight of a large reel of wire. All goes well until they reach the summit of a ridge, when, suddenly, a barrage from a "whizz bang" battery is placed right down on top of the party. There is nothing for it but to remain crouched in a friendly shell-hole, which affords a little protection, until the storm blows over or to risk the chances of being hit in the open. The journey is then resumed, and much relief is felt when at last the ground over a nasty dip is traversed without mishap, as this is known to be a favourite target for hostile gunners. A muddy, unkempt communication-trench is now entered, and the party proceed, up a slope, towards the support system, and eventually arrive at their destination—a post in the front line overlooking its objective. Difficulty is experienced in preserving the wire from the unguarded feet of infantrymen, who look askance at the party as it passes, cursing the idiosyncrasies of each fire bay. The instrument is connected with the end of the wire, and all hold their breath in order to hear the answering buzz which tells them that they are through to the battery. Several futile buzzes may be made by the telephonist, and then, no response being forthcoming, a linesman is sent down the wire towards the first relay station. A break in the wire is discovered and speedily mended, the next attempt is successful, and the battery is called to action.

During registration the wire often breaks, and serious delays occur, but, at length, the last gun is duly pronounced O.K. by the officer. Just in the nick of time, too! for the enemy commences a sharp retaliation on the portion of the trench occupied by the little party. Refuge is sought in an old enemy shaft close by, and there it awaits the time for the "show" to commence. Several other batteries also take part in the shoot, and it is quite impossible to pick out the shells which belong to each one as they fall. Complete success crowns the effort, but on the particular day here described the F.O.O. and party failed to see the end of the bout, as they were subjected to very heavy fire, and were all blown down the mouth of the shaft by the explosion of a shell. Luckily, though badly shaken, all escaped without injury.

Meanwhile (p. 035) the wire has been broken in many places and is beyond repair, but it has already served its purpose, and, when fire has died down, the party starts on the return journey. On arriving at the first relay station, the telephonist on duty is found dead at his post, the receiver still clutched in his hand and held to his ear. A nasty gash in the forehead reveals the place where he has been hit and instantly killed. His companion is nowhere to be found, although bloodstains denote that he has at least been wounded, and, on investigation, it is ascertained that the linesman has been hit, picked up by passing comrades, and taken to an aid-post. The journey is resumed, the party carrying the dead with them, and presently another hostile barrage is encountered. Again the men lie low until it ceases, and then pick up the remaining linesmen, and return to the battery utterly exhausted. Many questions are asked, and it frequently happens that the F.O.O. is cursed by his Battery Commander for not keeping the wire going, and even the Brigade joins in the chorus. The young officer pays little heed, and inwardly reflects that they should be extremely thankful that communication was established at all, and that those of the party who returned did so in safety. So, in spite of everything, he consumes a hearty dinner and retires to bed, sleeping the sleep of the just, and soon becomes oblivious of all his little worries and sombre surroundings.

Towards the middle of October the weather broke, and conditions became intolerable. The roads, which had been partially repaired, were still soft and broken, and developed into quagmires—mud and water to a depth of two and three feet made vehicular traffic almost out of the question. All ammunition had to be transported to the guns by means of horses carrying pack saddles, a slow and tedious method, which took a lot out of men and beasts alike. As yet no decca-ville railways had been constructed as far as battery positions. Very heavy work thus fell on those at the wagon lines, who were kept busy most of the day and night. Although the distance to the gun position was under five miles there and back, the journey rarely took less than ten hours to accomplish. If a horse fell down in this sticky mud, heavily laden as it was, attempts at rescue proved unavailing, except on rare occasions, even with the aid of drag-ropes, and the unfortunate animal had to be "dispatched." Was it a sense of humour that prompted those in authority to send the subalterns, in turn, to the wagon lines for a "rest"? Anyhow, it was considered (p. 036) anything but that by the poor unfortunates who went, and right glad they were when the time came round for their next period of duty with the guns!

As the weather rapidly became worse, operations came to a standstill, and all proceeded to dig themselves in for the coming winter. Every endeavour was made to make our quarters waterproof, as well as shell-proof, and some attempts at mining were commenced, but the condition of the ground was all against such an undertaking, and the work was abandoned. Then whispers spread abroad that we were to be relieved for a short rest, and, after ten weeks of incessant fighting, we were withdrawn from the line and marched to a little village named Hangest, a few miles west of Amiens. There we were glad to find ourselves installed in billets with a roof covering us once more. A week of leisure helped greatly to restore our spirits, and again we set out for the line. Our destination this time was Combles, and we took over a battery position from the French, who politely made us acquainted with our new surroundings. Our allies, who had been fighting side-by-side with us on our right flank throughout the great battle, were then withdrawn, and the British front was extended to the south as far as the banks of the River Somme. Evidence was speedily forthcoming to convince us of the severe nature of the recent fight. The ground was strewn with wreckage and material of all descriptions, and many hostile guns were found abandoned or lying where they had been put out of action by the irresistible dash of the Poilus.

The country, in this part, was undulating, and better suited to the concealment of battery positions, and nowhere was the enemy able to overlook our territory. Our area included the defence of the joint villages of Sailly-Saillisel, situated on commanding ground, which the French had recently bravely stormed. Combles, too, which lay in a basin shaped hollow, was interesting as having been the centre of supplies for the southern portion of the German Army operating in the battle, and much booty was discovered in the huge catacombs which ran underneath the town.

'Xmas passed in much the same way as in the previous year. A smart bombardment was carried out in the morning in order to advise the enemy that anything in the way of fraternising would not be countenanced by us. At mid-day the men partook of (p. 037) their 'Xmas fare, which had been fetched from Amiens, and a short service was conducted by the Padre in one of the gun-pits. A slight disturbance took place at dusk, when the S.O.S. went up from the front line and all batteries immediately opened out. It seemed a rather extraordinary occurrence, as the evening was unusually quiet, and, presently, it was discovered to have arisen through an error, due to the fact that the enemy had put up a coloured light in between two ordinary Verey lights which constituted our own S.O.S.

About this time the enemy caused considerable annoyance to a certain Battalion Headquarters, situated in a quarry close behind the lines, by occasionally dropping a shell right into it, the position having probably been discovered by his aircraft. Retaliation tactics were adopted, which consisted of subjecting the hostile trenches to a sharp half-hour's bombardment from eight batteries, firing a total of 2,000 rounds. The enemy was well known to be very thick-skinned, but these measures met with instant success, and it was only necessary to remind him once again that we were not to be trifled with in this way.

After the New Year, a severe spell of frost set in, with an occasional heavy fall of snow, and we were somewhat annoyed when orders came through to sideslip our position further south, as we had made our quarters fairly comfortable by this time, and expected to remain undisturbed throughout the winter. The new position was situated behind the ruined village of Rancourt, facing St. Pierre Vaast wood, and was one of the worst and most disagreeable localities it was ever our lot to occupy, as we were, more or less, waterlogged the whole of our time there. Much difficulty was experienced by both friend and foe in entering their respective front line, so much so that, by common consent, sniping by rifle fire was discontinued until parapets were constructed and made fit for occupation. However, sniping was still indulged in by the artillery, and no parties of any size were permitted to go about freely near the front line under observation. Affairs continued thus until the middle of February, when it became apparent that something unusual was taking place in enemy territory, and great explosions were heard, after which volumes of smoke were seen to rise in large columns.

These, as was afterwards proved, were due to preparations being made by the enemy to evacuate the low-lying country, into which they had reluctantly been forced, as the result of the battle of the Somme, (p. 038) prior to falling back upon the great prepared defences known as the Hindenburg Line.

Instantly every one was on the alert for further signs of evacuation, and one morning a patrol reported that the enemy had vacated their front line. Further patrols were at once pushed out, through St. Pierre Vaast wood, in order to maintain contact with the retreating foe. Every precaution had to be taken, as it was soon discovered that many forms of booby-traps had been cunningly laid by him in his wake, and progress was necessarily slow. Added to this, there was great difficulty in manœuvring the guns over the innumerable trenches which existed in the neighbourhood, and the pieces sank up to their axles in the clogging mud, and were only extricated after hours of labour. The enemy retired slowly and most methodically, destroying everything of value and wantonly reducing the small villages and hamlets to mere shells, by means of incendiary bombs. The inhabitants also were removed beforehand, and, when the troops advanced, they might have been traversing a wilderness, so complete was the ruin and desolation on all sides.

The time had now arrived for the Brigade to have a much-needed rest and also to refit, so, at the end of March, we were withdrawn from the contest. Marching westward, we arrived at the village of Morlancourt in the first week of April, well content at the prospect of returning to civilization for a protracted period.

"Division from Brigade R.F.A. Guards Division."

# CHAPTER VI. (p. 039)

**Messines.**

It was not long before those in authority discovered that the neighbourhood of Morlancourt was peculiarly favourable for the carrying out of manœuvres, with the result that a period of "intensive training" set in. Drill orders took place four days a week, and batteries were specially trained in the methods of open warfare, while many hours were devoted to tactical schemes.

At this time units were reorganised, all batteries were increased to six guns, and there was plenty of work to keep everyone busy. The narrator of these rambling notes, after a period of two years' service with the Brigade, here transferred his allegiance to the sister howitzer battery of the Division, known as "The Grey Battery," from the fact that all the horses were of that colour. Sentiment ran strong for his "old love" and those he was obliged to leave, but he was already well acquainted with both officers and men of his new unit, and soon settled down happily amongst them.

All guns were carefully calibrated on a range due west of Peronne, and the "hairies" picked up rapidly in condition, owing to the good care and attention that was bestowed upon them. The big battles of Vimy Ridge and Arras were now in full swing, and it seemed unlikely that we would be called upon to take any part in them so late in the day.

Many forms of amusement were created for the men, and football matches, both "rugger" and "soccer," were freely indulged in between batteries and brigades, while the full regimental band of one of the Guards' regiments was kindly lent to the Divisional Artillery. It gave many a fine entertainment in the evenings.

Time thus sped by at an amazing rate, and various visits of inspection paid us by officers from the C.R.A. up to the Army Commander (p. 040) made it very apparent that we were undoubtedly being "fattened up"—but for what? The question was more than we could answer, but speculations were rife as to our possible destination, for we knew that the Somme would see us no more—in the meantime, at all events.

Six weeks had come and gone, and yet we remained inactive in this peaceful village; then sudden orders were issued for us to be ready to entrain at short notice, and, in the second week of May, the Battery glided out of the station at Meulte prepared for anything. A long and circuitous route was taken *via* Amiens, Abbeville, Etaples, Boulogne, Calais, St. Omer, and at length we arrived at Arques, near which we remained, in billets, for some considerable time. It was while we were there that we learnt that it was the intention of the British Commander to gain possession of the great Messines Ridge, which towered over our lines, and was a stronghold of inestimable value to the enemy.

As long as he held this ridge, which was the keystone of his armies in Flanders, he was immune from any vulnerable attack on our part, and was free to launch any offensive operation from it by using it as a stepping-off place. Added to this, the northern end of the heights afforded him an uninterrupted view of the southern portion of the Ypres salient, which was a source of great annoyance to our forces on that part of the front. It was vital, therefore, for the future operations of the British Armies, that this important ridge should be captured and kept in our hands.

Preparations were accordingly set on foot, and artillery of all calibre was silently concentrated from all parts, and proceeded to dig itself in for the coming fray. For a long time this sector had been free from any serious operations, and was considered a kind of resting place for exhausted troops, but soon the peace and quiet of the neighbourhood was to receive a rude awakening, when the tide of battle broke out upon it once more.

Proceeding through Hazebrouck and Bailleul, the Brigade arrived at its wagon lines, a short distance west of Neuve Eglise, and immediately each battery sent work parties to the scene of action, in order to construct emplacements and make its position habitable. The spot allotted to our battery was in a little hollow close to the cut roads, near the small ruined village of Wulverghen. Our front line was placed on the top of an undulating rise, with the ridge itself beyond.

Our (p. 041) principal business was to avoid attracting the attention of the enemy to our preparations, and in this we were aided by the fact that there was a considerable amount of cover beside us, in the form of trees and undergrowth, the foliage of which was now in full leaf.

Row upon row of batteries were placed in position behind hedges, or artificially concealed, the barrels of the pieces peeping out from all imaginable lurking places. The Divisional Artillery was situated in the most advanced position, the 18 pr. batteries ranging from within 600 to 1,000 yards of the front line, with the howitzer batteries immediately behind them. On account of our proximity to the enemy, the two brigades had orders to remain silent until the day of the show, and we were only allowed to fire enough rounds to enable us to carefully register the pieces, and this was completed without giving away any of the positions.

All ammunition was conveyed to the guns by night, and was distributed in small quantities near to them. Before long the enemy became alive to the fact that we were contemplating some move, and consequently increased his devastating fire by night, with the result that many dumps in the vicinity were exploded by him. He was bound to hit something, the countryside was so packed with all manner of ammunition. He had no idea, however, of the magnitude of our coming effort, and firmly believed his position to be impregnable, and that it was beyond our power to free ourselves from his grip.

He contented himself with drenching our little valley with chemical shell whenever conditions were favourable, but so accustomed were the men to their gas masks that no serious consequences resulted, although it was distinctly unpleasant to have to pass each night enveloped in these stuffy contrivances, especially as the weather remained hot and oppressive.

The Battery had more than their average share of good fortune throughout these operations, and it is worthy of putting on record that the unit did not sustain a single casualty to either man or horse. This was all the more remarkable as the engineers had constructed a wide plank road, which passed through the centre of our position, and could not be concealed from our foes, who lavishly besprinkled it with shrapnel after dark. Many casualties were caused to the transport, and the Officers' Mess virtually became an aid-post, where every assistance was rendered the wounded men.

Our (p. 042) sister howitzer battery was lined up alongside of us, and, when the two positions were first inspected, much chaff ensued as to which had the better place, and the men of our battery were certainly all of the opinion that, had the selection devolved upon them, we would unanimously have plumped for the other one. They had no landmarks likely to attract hostile fire, and thus occasion them the unpleasant sensation of living on top of a volcano, while we were slap-bang in the middle of a conspicuous cross road, with a constant stream of traffic coming and going through: yet, so strange and fickle are the fortunes of war that, while we escaped unharmed, our comrades next door suffered a heavy gruelling.

The preliminary bombardment commenced, and continued throughout five days, but, in order to deceive the enemy as to our weight of artillery, not more than fifty per cent. of the guns in the line were allowed to take part at one time. A row of O.P.'s had been constructed on Hill 65, which overlooked the valley and town of Messines. A fine sight was witnessed as that stronghold was gradually reduced to a mere shell by our heavies, which effected extraordinarily good work in smashing the elaborate structures of the enemy's defence.

The preparations were all that could be desired, and everything was carefully worked out to the minutest detail: not a stone was left unturned to render the operations a complete success. The labour and expense was well rewarded too, for surely no battle ever ran so smoothly from first to last, and it will always be looked back upon by the British soldier as a model of triumphant organisation. The battle only lasted a single day, but in that time the formidable network of trenches was neatly and clearly shorn off, and the enemy, who relied so much on the security of these positions, found himself suddenly pushed down the slope into unsuitable ground, where he could no longer be a menace to us.

The "feet" of our Division were not in the line, being held in reserve, and, as it turned out, they were not called upon at all at this juncture, so well did the course of the battle progress. We were covering the infantry of an English Division, and, on the evening previous to the attack, the troops passed us noiselessly and in perfect order on their way to their various points of assembly. All were in excellent spirits, which augured well for the next day, and a feeling of calm confidence appeared to prevail (p. 043) amongst them. A stream of gas and tear shells was maintained by the foe throughout the night, but it was mostly directed on the zone which contained the battery positions, consequently the infantry was caused little inconvenience.

Early the following morning, shortly before dawn, the attack was heralded by the explosion of the mines, which had been in course of preparation for months beforehand. This was the sign for the guns to open out, and the assault was launched from north of St. Eloi in the Salient to the neighbourhood of Ploegsterte in the south, the men following close in the wake of the now familiar and popular creeping barrage.

The force of the explosions was terrific, and the vibration was felt far and wide; even strong concrete "pill-boxes" were swung to and fro, and the occupants were tossed from side to side as if they were on board ship in a rough sea. Some indication of the colossal nature of these upheavals may be gauged from the fact that the craters were, in some cases, more than 200 ft. in diameter, and that the earth thrown up obliterated every hostile trench in the vicinity, completely burying the unfortunate garrisons who manned them.

At the same moment the sky was lit up by all manner of S.O.S. lights and the innumerable flashes from our guns, which were now showing their maximum strength for the first time. They belched forth concentrated death, the roar reached such a deafening crescendo that conversation was entirely out of the question — indeed it was impossible to hear one's own voice. However, the scene was truly impressive, and the grandeur was beyond anything hitherto seen.

As daylight crept in, the infantry were observed to be making rapid progress, although, here and there, stiff opposition was encountered. Soon the summit of the ridge was gained, and the men swept on and disappeared over the crest, leaving the mopping-up parties to complete their work. The Tanks bravely waddled up after them, in a vain effort to keep up, for the attacking infantry went so fast, in the first stages, that they easily outstripped those ponderous giants and left them far behind.

Meanwhile the field batteries which had been in position farthest in the rear, and so were already out of range, limbered up and dashed into action in front of our Brigade. As soon as the next row was also out of action, they too galloped past (p. 044) and took up their place again in "No Man's Land," while the Engineers worked at their highest pressure to pull down trenches and prepare the way for the gunners. Thus we were able to give the fullest possible support to the infantry, and the fire never ceased, while the men always found the creeping barrage laid down in front of them.

Early on in the fray prisoners came dribbling back in a more or less dazed condition, and, as they passed the array of guns, they paused and gazed in evident wonder at the huge concentration—probably realising how fortunate they were in escaping the fate of so many of their comrades.

Now, the enemy, although he knew an attack was imminent, had failed to anticipate the correct zero day, with the result that, on several portions of this front, various reliefs were in process of taking place at the actual time of the assault. The consequence was his defence was thrown into a state of confusion, while the extra numbers in the trench offered a double prey for the bayonets of our men, who were not slow in seizing the chances thus afforded them.

The whole of the first objectives were quickly in our possession, as well as the villages of Messines and Wytscheate, and there was a slight pause to give a breathing space to the infantry, and to allow time for the field guns to take up their allotted positions beyond the recently captured enemy trenches, before entering upon the second and final stage of the battle. When the creeping barrage, which had remained stationary during this period, went forward once more, the infantry encountered stronger opposition, but by this time the Tanks were well up in support, and were instrumental in breaking up the machine-gun nests and thus enabling the men to proceed up to schedule time.

The enemy lost a number of field artillery pieces, but had taken the precaution to withdraw most of the heavy ones several days before, when our bombardment commenced. His shooting, therefore, was rather wild and erratic, as he evidently had not had sufficient time to register his guns properly in the new positions. The result was that, fortunately for us, most of his energy was misplaced, and, for a battle of this magnitude, the casualties were not as heavy as might have been expected.

By (p. 045) early afternoon the final objectives were everywhere in our hands, and the work of consolidating the fruitful gains that the last few hours had yielded was immediately begun.

Several counter-attacks were attempted by the enemy, but were not pushed with much vigour, and no success was secured in that direction: our infantry remained firm and could not be dislodged.

Trenches were swiftly constructed, the work proceeding without intermission, and by evening the men were, more or less, securely "dug in," except in a few places where the line was slightly irregular, and which was afterwards rectified by means of a small operation.

By the time the battle had finished we found ourselves the farthest back Brigade in the line, the immense number of batteries which, at the beginning, had been in our rear were now well in front of us, and on this sector the Divisional Artillery were the only two Brigades who did not move forward during the course of the fight. Moreover, by this time we were firing almost at extreme range close to the enemy's new front line, which gives some idea of the distance our men covered.

The day had been an exhausting one for the gunners, and, in order to give some indication of the work and labour they had been called upon to do, our battery alone fired over 4000 rounds of ammunition. This was by no means a bad performance when one takes into consideration that each shell weighs 35 lbs., and necessitated a goodly amount of manhandling, but the men all had their "peckers well up," and displayed much determination throughout.

For a few days following the battle there were a number of small isolated scraps for positions, and one or two enemy counter-attacks, before the new front settled down into something like normal conditions again. Decca-ville and light railways were pushed up smartly by the R.O.D., and the Engineers constructed new roads, while Labour Battalions were busily employed repairing the old ones and clearing up the litter of the battlefield.

Ever since we came into action it had been no secret that our stay in this area would be of short duration, and that we were only to be employed in the battle itself, and were only to remain as long as our services were really required. (p. 046) It was no surprise when, five days later, orders came through for us to withdraw from the line. We pulled out back to our wagon line, and from there proceeded through Bailleul to the little hamlet of Borre, a few miles east of Hazebrouck, where we remained pending removal to our next destination. We all had the feeling that our recent tour had been a great success, and were well satisfied with the part we had taken in the operations, for this was the first occasion on which we had witnessed a battle go smoothly, without a hitch from start to finish, and was a great contrast to any previous one in which we had participated.

A few days in rest sufficed to put the Brigade shipshape once more, and we were now ready for the next bout. No delay was made in transferring us to another neighbourhood, and we set out in a northerly direction, which boded little good, for we knew that unpleasant events were developing in that quarter.

# CHAPTER VII. (p. 047)

## Ypres Again.

In the middle of June the Division arrived in the neighbourhood of Ypres, and at once took over from the Belgians from just below Boesinghe northwards. We were thus back on familiar ground, as we had occupied the next sector to the south in the previous year. Although we were not actually in the Salient itself, we were situated at the northern re-entrant to it. The Yser Canal constituted "No Man's Land," the eastern bank of which was held by the enemy and the western by ourselves.

The battery positions on this occasion were placed a considerable distance behind, mainly around the village of Elverdinghe, as the enemy had close observation and overlooked us from Pilkem Ridge. We did not take long to discover that our opponents were well acquainted with the situation of our new homes, for the majority of the batteries were subjected at once to an avalanche of shells as soon as they opened fire in order to register the guns. It became imperative for us to build alternative positions or go elsewhere, while other sections moved forward and undertook most of the firing. We had not been settled more than a few days when the enemy suddenly conceived a violent attraction for the house occupied by the officers' mess, and, after several direct hits had been made on it, we decided that the place was becoming too hot, and searched round for a more suitable abode. We packed up, made a hasty flight, and secured accommodation in a house which was strengthened by concrete, but even there we had to be wary, especially at night, for we were very close to a road fork, beloved by the enemy gunners.

The majority of the O.P.'s were also obvious to the keen eyes of the foe, who paid them much attention on every possible occasion, and it was just as well for the occupants that (p. 048) they had been strongly constructed with steel girders and concrete. On one occasion an officer, doing a night O.P. duty, along with his telephonist, was subjected to a full hour's bombardment by two hostile batteries, which fired salvoes regularly every minute. Next morning there was nothing left of the house except the skeleton, with the O.P. structure standing out defiant in bold relief in the midst of it.

These then were the conditions on this sector at the time of our taking it over, and it will be seen that the enemy did more or less what he chose, and was undoubtedly top dog as far as gunnery was concerned. However, this was not to remain long so, as almost immediately preparations were set on foot for the coming offensive, which had already been decided upon.

A host of new O.P.'s were erected, new roads and light railways constructed, while large working parties prepared fresh gun pits in advanced positions, and all were carefully camouflaged where they were exposed to enemy view. Every day new units arrived, and the country appeared to be overrun with troops. Most of the forward work had to be done during the night, and, as each position was completed, the guns were silently concentrated. While this was in progress, the Divisional Artillery only were maintained for the defence of the line, as it was not advisable that the enemy should know until the last possible moment that anything unusual was afoot. The scheme was a much more ambitious one than that in which we had recently taken a part, and, if everything went forward according to plan, it meant that we would be on the go for a considerable time, and there even appeared to be a chance of getting a taste of the long-talked-of open warfare.

About this time a most amusing episode was witnessed by one of our Subalterns who was doing a liaison with the infantry at a battalion headquarters. This place was situated most unpleasantly, and was well known to the enemy, consequently accommodation had to be sought underground as much as possible. While the F.O.O. and his companion, the Intelligence Officer, were performing their ablutions early one morning outside the mouth of the cellar, a Brigadier with his Staff suddenly appeared on the scene to pay a visit to the Commander. The two Staff Officers remained outside, and opened (p. 049) conversation with them. The Intelligence Officer, being something of a wag, brandished his shaving brush in one hand and with the other jocularly shoved the Staff Captain down the steps into their retreat, and asked him what he thought of the bedchamber. The other officer, although much amused, stood aghast, and, after the visitors had departed, he asked his companion to whom he had been speaking. He replied that he did not know, for, although the Captain's features appeared familiar, he could not "place" him, though he was a jolly sort of chap anyhow. On being told that it was none other than the Prince of Wales that he had been familiarly digging in the ribs for the past quarter of an hour, he was incredulous, and exclaimed, "And to think I nearly killed the youngster down these stairs!"

At length preparations were completed, and the two Brigades of the Divisional Artillery took up new advanced positions alongside the reinforcing batteries already in line, while the heavies were thickly aligned close in the rear. The preliminary bombardment broke out about the middle of July, and at first it was keenly resented by the enemy, who perceived that we were gradually wrestling the initiative from him, but when, day after day, our fire continued unabated, he apparently resigned himself to his fate. Hurricane shoots by field batteries soon began to make a difference in the appearance of his trenches, and the heavies, by means of aerial registration, demolished his strongholds far back over the crest, and destroyed many of his battery positions. Several thick woods were facing us across the canal, and these grew thinner, and yet more thin, disclosing cunningly concealed pill-boxes, which were then dealt with by the heavies, until at last only a few stumps remained to indicate that a wood had ever existed there. The enemy's alarm grew daily, and soon our aeroplanes reported that the hostile batteries were being withdrawn further out of danger, and that work was proceeding feverishly upon new defences far behind his lines. By this time we had complete control of the air, and the heavens were alive with our aircraft, though the enemy tried his best to equalise matters by bringing along his famous "travelling circus" to the scene of action, and many thrilling fights were witnessed. The batteries were subjected to much chemical shelling during the night, and the enemy were known to bring forward special guns (p. 050) under cover of darkness for this purpose, and to withdraw them out of range again before daybreak.

It was during this period that he introduced the new mustard gas for the first time, and it must be admitted that he surprised and inflicted considerable casualties on us at first by this latest specimen in his assortment of poison.

Our initial attack had to be postponed for several days, as the French, who came in immediately on our left, were delayed in putting in their appearance, consequently they had many hours' bombardment to make up, but, when it did commence, it was no uncertain one, and the noise was terrific. In the meantime our bombardment was continued also, though in a lesser degree, and the destruction of the enemy's lines was, as far as we were able to judge, thorough and complete.

This delay proved a blessing in disguise to the Guards, who were to deliver the assault on our sector. The problem of effecting a crossing of the canal was a most serious and difficult one, and it had been arranged to send the men over on floating mats, as a good deal of water still remained in parts of the bed. In others so much mud and slime were encountered, while carrying out a series of raids, that it was almost impossible to cross without some such assistance, and it will be readily understood that it was imperative to waste no time in this manoeuvre, especially as the foe was awaiting them on the further bank. Whether it was that the enemy could not maintain communications between his front line and the rear, on account of our intense bombardment, or whether, as has been suggested, he suspected a repetition of Messines, and that we had mined underneath the canal bed, at all events three days before the attack he evacuated the canal bank and retired just over the crest of the hill some 800 yards beyond. This movement, however, had not been carried out unperceived by our valiant airmen, who, flying at a low altitude, returned and reported the situation. Immediately strong patrols crossed the canal and pushed up the slope on the other side, in order to remain in contact with the enemy and gauge his whereabouts. A series of posts were thus established 500 to 600 yards east of the canal, and orders were given to hold them at all costs, so that on the day of the battle our infantry could start off from there without having any serious obstacle in their way. Many men crossed the canal by means of hastily constructed foot bridges or floating rafts made of biscuit and petrol tins ingeniously lashed together.

On (p. 051) this occasion we will follow the fortunes of the F.O.O.'s detailed to accompany the infantry on their journey over the top on the first day of the battle. The party consisted of two officers and fourteen signallers and linesmen from the Brigade, who, during the past fortnight, had received full instructions as to their duties. Every detail had been carefully worked out beforehand: the men had been divided into several groups, each armed with telephones, reels of wire, flags, and Lucas lamps, all these things being necessary for the provision of each relay station. One of the officers was to accompany the attacking waves of infantry with his staff, consisting of a telephonist, linesman, and signaller, while the duty of the other was to work in conjunction with him and to maintain, as far as possible, uninterrupted communication with the Brigade after laying down the wire. The morning before the battle, the wire was laid out over the canal as far as the series of outposts, in order to save time on the following day. The same evening, at sunset, the party set out, after receiving wishes for the best of good luck from those who had been fortunate enough to escape being detailed for this arduous task. Officers and men proceeded to their appointed places in the front line, or rather in what had once been an enemy support trench, though now it was scarcely recognisable as such, owing to the effects of our bombardment, there to remain for the night and await coming events.

Now, in consequence of the enemy's premature retirement over the crest, he lost most of his observation on us, but he was aware we had effected a crossing and held posts on his side of the canal. He therefore lavishly besprinkled this area with all manner of high explosive shells—one here, one there: never two in the same place—and the members of the party began to wonder whether they would survive to witness the fortunes of the battle. It always appears to be a matter of conjecture as to what are the real feelings of an F.O.O. about to take the plunge, so perhaps it might be of interest in this case to acquaint ourselves with them. As he lies out there with his men, where are his thoughts? Are they of his home, his parents, wife, or children? Will he ever see their dear faces again? No—! all that agony has been fought out over and over again long ago, during the previous fortnight or so, since he has been detailed for this particular job. Then, what does he think about? If the truth be told, he is rapidly running over in his mind all the little things which may (p. 052) perhaps, at the last moment, have been omitted or forgotten. He questions Gunner "So-and-so" to make certain that that extra piece of wire has been brought along, and asks what the h—l Gunner "Somebody else" is doing standing there without a "tin-hat" on, and enquires of the Bombardier if he has adjusted the Lucas lamp properly, which has been giving some trouble previously. These and a hundred-and-one other such questions flash through his brain as he lies on the ground with his little party, all vigorously puffing pipes or cigarettes. The hours go by very slowly, and conversation on any old topic is attempted from time to time, sleep being entirely out of the question, as everyone is much too excited for anything of that nature. Meanwhile the bombardment continues without intermission, and the night becomes intensely cold and eerie. Will the darkness never pass and let us get started on the job?

Soon after midnight the infantry, who are to make the assault, arrive at their places of assembly, full of quips and jests, a sure sign that they are cheery and in good form for the coming fray. Rum is served out, and the men lie down in little bunches, either to snatch a few minutes' sleep or else to resume their constant arguments and bickerings on every subject under the sun except anything connected with the war. Zero hour at last draws near, and everyone grows more restless, for this period is much the most trying time to endure, and all topics of conversation have long since been exhausted. Then a short, sharp order passes down the line, and the answering shouts announce that all are present and ready—the "quarter to zero" has arrived. Another crisp order comes along, and there are a series of ominous clicks as each man adjusts his bayonet to the rifle, then the men line up in perfect extended order, ready for the word to go. A faint grey appears in the sky to the east, but only the next man is visible to his neighbour, as the darkness is still upon us. The F.O.O.'s and party are also up and ready, final instructions being rapidly given to the signallers, who nod assent that everything is prepared and understood. Then suddenly the guns bark out afresh, and a creeping barrage drops down like a curtain in front of the men, who follow after it at an easy walk. Fortune attends the little party, as the wire has only been cut in three places, and these are speedily repaired; and, as soon as the second wave of men is clear of the trench, the line is laid out as rapidly as possible behind them. The ground is difficult to traverse, (p. 053) being full of deep craters, so the party progresses more slowly than the infantry, and presently the third wave gains on and passes it by. At first the enemy puts down a nasty barrage, just beyond our stepping-off place, but most of his heavy stuff falls on the canal bank, and, as the majority of the troops have already crossed, the damage is not severe. By this time the party has gained the top of the crest, and, after establishing a relay station in a pill-box lately occupied by their opponents, the remainder proceed on their way. Many are the temptations to dawdle, instead of getting on with the work, so much of interest is taking place around them, including the amusing, and at that time not too frequent, sight of scores of the enemy, with uplifted hands, emerging from pill boxes, where they must have been packed like sardines.

An auxiliary wire tapped into the main F.O.O. line is led to another pill-box, now to be used as a new infantry headquarters for the time being, and the party comes under the fire of a hostile machine gun emplacement, which necessitates their lying in a shellhole for a while. On arrival there, the "mopping up" party is found still at work, but it soon completes its grim task. The officer who has proceeded with the infantry now sends his first message through to the effect that the first objectives are taken, the wire fortunately holding out well at the moment, every sound being clear and distinct. The Lucas lamp is then fixed on top of the relay station, and communications established in case the wire goes, but the morning dawns in mist, and signalling by this method is unsatisfactory.

After a short pause, the infantry proceed on the second stage of their adventure, the F.O.O. and party following up and laying out wire close behind them. More messages are sent through to Brigade, and the wire breaks on several occasions, but is speedily dealt with by the linesmen, who are kept busy patrolling up and down the line. Meanwhile, items of extreme interest are taking place around the pill-pox of the Central Relay Station. Numerous batches of prisoners are drifting back, for the most part unattended, composed entirely of youths of nineteen and twenty years of age, the Guards having refused to kill these babies, only "despatching" the older men, for the Division up against them was very mixed, and may best be described as a "dud" lot, and it did not put up much of a fight. The lads all look weary and mud-stained, although there is an expression of relief (p. 054) on their faces, as they steadily munch the bread that has been good-naturedly handed to them by their captors, for they have been starving for the past three days or so, no food having reached them on account of the terrific bombardment. An aid-post is hastily placed in a huge shell-hole close by, and the wounded straggle back; those who are but slightly hit and can walk help each other along, while the others are carried on stretchers. Here, a man, ghastly wounded, minus one leg and with the other almost severed, lies on a stretcher, calmly puffing at a cigarette given him by the bearers, and attempts to raise himself on his elbow that he may gaze at the curious scenes taking place around him. Others just stagger along, their pinched faces showing signs of suppressed pain, yet all have a quip or a jest on their lips as they smoke the inevitable cigarette. The sight is truly a wonderful one! The courage and calm that these wounded display in the midst of their sufferings is beyond words, but they are "Greatheart's all." Reinforcements are passing all this time on their way up to the battle line, ready to throw themselves into the conflict when their time arrives.

Again the infantry move forward to the third and final objective, under cover of the friendly barrage, and, by the time they arrive at their allotted destination, an advance of some three miles from the canal bank has been effected since morning. The wire is linked up, and the F.O.O. selects a good point of vantage, and makes himself and his staff as comfortable as possible, and then proceeds to gather as much information as he can obtain to send back over the line. The infantry are now busy digging themselves in, and are being subjected to heavy shell-fire, but they stubbornly resist all efforts to dislodge them. By this time the batteries have all limbered up and advanced to new positions, mostly out in the open, and an order comes over the telephone from the B.C.'s for the F.O.O. to register the guns afresh: so he at once picks up some dependable landmark, and with much difficulty observes the rounds as they fall, and thus gives the necessary corrections.

Then the wires break on account of the shelling, and some time is lost before communications are again established. The enemy has now recovered somewhat from the initial shock of the attack, and displays much determination to recover lost ground—counter attacks are launched without success. The F.O.O. now has an important message to convey, but, when the telephonist (p. 055) endeavours to send it through, there is no answering buzz. Thereupon the linesman is despatched as a runner, and, on reaching the first relay station, he transfers the written message to another linesman, who immediately sets out for the next relief, and so on, until the message duly arrives at headquarters.

Thus the day wears on: sometimes direct communication is possible, and at others the wire is "dished," but, on the whole, a good deal of information is passed through. The relay posts are constantly shelled, and the bombardier in charge is wounded, while one runner was killed in his gallant endeavour to pass through a heavy barrage with an important communication. In the evening the party, much exhausted with the strenuous and never ending work of the day, is relieved by a fresh group of officers and signallers, who take over from them, and the little party wind their way homewards profoundly thankful to find themselves back with their unit safe and sound.

The situation, at the end of the opening day of the battle, was roughly this: — In the north all had gone well, and most of the objectives aimed at were successfully taken, but, such stiff resistance was met with further south, that the assaulting troops were held up after they had gained only about half of those allotted to them, and, although they fought stubbornly and determinedly, they were unable to make further ground. Thus the left wing was forced to mark time while the troops on the right made a series of attacks in order to straighten out the line, otherwise the army to the north would have found itself enclosed in a nasty salient. The artillery, over the whole battle front, also encountered great difficulty in advancing the guns, the ground was so ploughed up by the effects of the long preliminary bombardment. Even the horse gunners, who were detailed to move up in immediate support of the infantry, were unable to proceed further than a few hundred yards on the other side of the canal. Huge craters, placed lip to lip, met them in all directions, and an advance was found to be out of the question till new tracks were prepared and the road cleared of debris. This naturally took some time to accomplish, and, meanwhile, all the field batteries were advanced as close to the canal bank as possible, but even then they were much too far behind, and were firing at almost extreme range.

No (p. 056) serious attack could be delivered, therefore, for some ten days, until sufficient time had elapsed to enable the gunners to occupy new positions some way across the canal, and, on this occasion, Langemarke fell into our hands, as well as the line of the Broombeke. Progress remained slow further south, consequently our front became stationary. Now, it so happened that most of our batteries were in extremely awkward positions, as we had expected to be moved forward at any time. They were right out in the open, devoid of any cover, and, for the most part, placed in shell holes which had been hastily converted into pits. Here we were subjected to the most "gruelling" time that was ever our lot to endure, and the battle developed into a gigantic duel between batteries, in which our position was no worse than the others. We lived in shell holes, scantily covered with corrugated iron and a layer or two of sandbags, scarcely splinter proof, nor had we any means of making ourselves more secure. The enemy's heavy counter batteries swept and searched over the slope where the majority of our batteries were congregated, and never before or after were they seen to reach such a pitch of efficiency.

Never a day passed without casualties, and often a number of gunners were buried as the result of an explosion, and had to be hastily dug out, and early on we lost one of our subaltern officers, who was borne away to the dressing station with no less than a dozen wounds on him. It was with great difficulty that the battery was kept in action sometimes, and, though we soon shifted our position to a flank, this did not relieve the situation. A 60 pdr. battery not far behind us developed the fatal habit of becoming particularly active during "flash time," and, as its flash was notoriously conspicuous, it was not surprising that its location was promptly pin-pointed by the enemy, who proceeded to knock it out: and this they succeeded in doing without much delay. During this particular contest we always got the short rounds, and, as they were not peas that were coming over, but 8" and 11" shells, the atmosphere was unpleasant, to say the least of it!

We considered ourselves lucky if we could keep 50 per cent. of the guns in action at the same time, while every nerve was strained to dig out the remainder, and it was a very heartless job, as a gun had no sooner been recovered and (p. 057) set up in position than it was knocked out again almost immediately. One morning, after a wild night of shelling by the enemy, on going to ascertain the damage, we found one gun with its barrel buried deep in the ground, the trail standing perpendicular pointing towards the sky; another completely turned over on its back pointing in the opposite direction, while a third had been blown right out of the shell hole in which it had been placed, and hurled a considerable distance away. Casualties to our establishment mounted at a most alarming rate, and one night our B.C. was mortally wounded by a high explosive shell, and, although such assistance as it was possible to give was rendered, he did not survive long after reaching the casually clearing station. His loss was much felt, not only by reason of his own cheerful personality, but also on account of the way in which he inspired all those under him to do their utmost, especially in times of stress and danger, when he always proved himself a true leader. The Captain now succeeded to the command of the battery, and the Senior Subaltern became second-in-command. It soon became evident that we could not carry on much longer under these conditions, and in the last week of September we were pulled out to refit, and remained near the village of Herszeele for a few days before again entering the fray.

Meanwhile a subaltern with a working party was busily occupied preparing new emplacements for our reception, and on the day of their completion he was wounded while riding his bicycle back to his billet: thus we lost yet another officer. But, try as we would, it was impossible to escape the vigilant eye of the enemy, who engaged battery positions one after another, and the number of guns knocked out was prodigious. Through a lucky chance it had been decided to take the guns "in" at dawn, instead of during the night, and by reason of this we escaped a most violent hostile bombardment which was directed against the position, and which damaged at least two of the pits and completely destroyed several dug-outs which the work party had recently striven so hard to build. We set to work and repaired most of the damage, and, whether or not it was the enemy thought he had disposed of us thereby, at all events he did not repeat the performance beyond subjecting us to the ordinary night harassing fire.

Another (p. 058) attack was impending, which again necessitated the forward movement of all batteries, and this time we were more fortunate in the selection of a site, and had several German pill-boxes in which to live and take refuge. Owing to the congestion on the one and only good road in the neighbourhood and the hostile shelling thereof, it was a matter of luck to find ourselves safely installed behind Abri Wood, and we immediately set out preparing for the new fight. Unfortunately, the weather again came to the assistance of our foe, and a spell of rain and wind made conditions extremely difficult for both infantry and gunners. However, the battle was proceeded with, and the result was an advance over the mud and slime of the river Broombeke as far as the outskirts of Houthoulst Forest, a distance of about two miles; our French allies, on the left, keeping in step with us throughout this operation. Then the inevitable forward move of the batteries was resumed, and this time we occupied positions down the further slope of the hill immediately across the rivulet of the Steenbeke. In consequence of torrents of rain, which continued daily, the low-lying ground became flooded, and it was all we could do to prevent the guns sinking in the sodden earth, and they frequently disappeared in the mud up to their axles. Dry accommodation was nowhere to be found except in a great pill-box, which we added to and strengthened, and it was popularly called the "Rabbit Hutch," for the obvious reason that it held the majority of the four batteries of the Brigade.

Now, our last attack had advanced us considerably further than the men on the right, who throughout the past month had encountered very stiff opposition, so we had perforce to remain stationary and mark time, while the battle continued to the south. On several occasions we rendered assistance by putting up what is commonly known as a "Chinese barrage," *i.e.*, the artillery carries out the ordinary programme preceding an attack, but no action follows on the part of the infantry. Conditions were equally disagreeable at the wagon lines, which speedily developed into quagmires, and it was almost impossible to walk about the lines unless attired in waders, and, even then, there was always the possibility of completely disappearing in the mud. Over and above that, the wagon lines were subjected every now and then to the attentions (p. 059) of a high velocity gun, as well as frequent visits from hostile night bombing machines, which were following the example set by our airmen and were endeavouring to pay us back in our own coin. Much damage was done in and around the neighbourhood, but our lines escaped exceedingly lightly. The question of ammunition supply became acute, and the use of pack saddles was again necessitated, and, because of the great distance between wagon lines and gun position, the round journey sometimes took eighteen hours to accomplish, and naturally the strain eventually told greatly upon both men and horses.

The battery positions were not long in being located by the enemy, who expended great quantities of ammunition in his attempts to destroy them: and he made much use of chemical and mustard shell, which in time saturated the low-lying ground on which the guns were placed. In this way he effectively gassed the B.C., a subaltern, and several of the men, who were all despatched to the wagon line, and the Captain assumed command for the time being and brought up reliefs with him. By this time the Battery was again in a very bad way, and a rest was promised on several occasions, only to be held up time and again with the exhortation to hold out yet a little while longer. Winter was rapidly approaching, and it was necessary to adjust our line before fighting came to a standstill: and a considerable distance had yet to be traversed before the goal — Passchendaele and the ridge on which it was situated — could be reached.

The battery, meanwhile, waited on in patience. All the remaining officers were affected by the mustard gas, as well as the majority of the gunners, and a sorry sight we presented when, in the first week in November, an incoming battery took over from us. We then proceeded to the new wagon lines, near Proven, in an utterly exhausted condition.

# CHAPTER VIII. (p. 060)

## Cambrai.

Everyone thought that our long-expected rest was now forthcoming, so it was a great surprise when we were ordered to hold ourselves in readiness for a long march.

What did it all mean? Were we marching into our new area and having our rest there or were we to be pitchforked into another scrap?

No indication of our destination was given, and everything seemed most mysterious: and, when the Brigade arrived in the neighbourhood of Merville, there did not appear to be any sign of a definite halt. At all events the journey was being performed in easy stages, as if we were filling in time, and we were always making further south, till, passing behind Bethune, the vicinity of Arras was reached. Here news of the surprise attack at Cambrai first reached our ears, the secret of which had been kept so well, and, heading in the direction of Bapaume, we were acquainted with the fact that we were again "for it."

Now, the initial attack, which came as a complete surprise to the enemy, had met with instant success, and, with the aid of a considerable number of Tanks, the great Hindenburg line had been breeched over a distance of from 6 to 8 miles, with the result that the fall of Cambrai a centre of great importance to the Germans appeared imminent.

However, after the first couple of days, the attack was not pressed home as it might have been, for some reason or other, and the fight came to an abrupt standstill, leaving our troops in a particularly baggy salient. These were the conditions that prevailed when the Division gradually moved nearer the scene of action.

In the beginning of the fourth week of November, we entered the battle, taking over from a famous Scottish Division which had fought with great distinction on the opening days.

The (p. 061) battery was placed in action to the north of Flesquieres, well inside the salient facing Bourlon Wood, in a position only recently completed by the enemy and which had not even been occupied by him. There was plenty of accommodation for everyone in the deep mined dug-outs prepared by him some thirty to forty feet below the ground, and the officers' quarters were spacious and lavishly constructed.

From this point the domes and the spires of the city of Cambrai could be clearly distinguished; indeed, they appeared such a short distance away, it looked as if a saunter would carry us into the heart of the town.

It was most interesting and instructive studying the elaborate system of the Hindenburg defences. First, there were three separate belts of closely-entwined barbed wire, each being some thirty yards wide, and behind them came a deep, narrow forefield trench that was only intended to be lightly manned. Communication trenches led back to the main Hindenburg trench some distance behind, in most cases being out of immediate view from our lately occupied positions.

This trench was both deep and wide, being some twelve feet across and duck-boarded throughout, raised on wooden stakes to prevent the water reaching the level of the pathway. At short intervals shafts led down to the spacious dug-outs beneath, which were all connected and linked up with one another. In fact, practically speaking, one could walk from one end of the line to the other below the surface of the ground.

Skilfully concealed, at frequent intervals, were emplacements for both trench-mortars and machine-guns, all heavily concreted and covered on top with turf.

The enemy must have thought himself very secure in this vast stronghold, but in a way this very fact contributed, in a great measure, to his undoing; for, it is common knowledge that the more one frequents deep dug-outs the less inclination there is to emerge from them when a scrap is taking place.

Finally, some 500 yards in the rear, a support line ran along, which, though not constructed with the same strength, was formidable enough in itself.

To judge by the indescribable mess, and by the mass of material left littered about, the enemy must indeed have beat a hasty retreat. The dug-outs were filthy to the last degree, and there was no sign of any system of sanitation having been used (p. 062) by these people, who considered their "Kultur" to be superlative, and who desired to impose it on the rest of mankind. All through the campaign, whenever one had the opportunity of inspecting hostile trenches and billets, one always found the same thing, filth and lack of sanitation.

Now, for some little time our hold on Bourlon Wood had been precarious, so a further attack was initiated, and the Guards went in to straighten the line. They swept through the Wood, taking the villages of Bourlon and Fontaine, but a gigantic counter attack pressed them back again owing to reinforcements being late in arriving to render assistance. They were so badly mauled and cut up that it was necessary to withdraw them from the line to refit, and infantry from an "Old Contemptible" Division took their place. Bourlon Wood became so saturated with gas that, after a great tussle, neither side was able to tenant it any longer, and so withdrew, leaving a screen of outposts to prevent any surprise attack.

This was the situation when dawn broke on the 30th of November, a day which proved to be one of ups and downs for us, and caused many misgivings to arise in the old country. The object of the enemy was to pinch either side of the jaws, and, if his attack on the north had met with equal success with that on the south, there would have been little hope for the troops in the salient, who undoubtedly would have been surrounded and cut off. However, as events turned out, our men held out and remained firm. Moreover, it was afterwards discovered from captured documents that the enemy's scheme was a large and ambitious one. Not only was it his intention to retake the whole of our recent gains, but to press on further through Havrincourt Wood, and establish himself on a line beyond it.

The Germans employed the same tactics as we used on the opening day of the battle — there was no preliminary bombardment, and their troops advanced under cover of a heavy mist and preceded by a creeping barrage. They put an overwhelming number of troops into the fight, the odds against our men being something like three to one, but our infantry in the north fought valiantly, although they were forced to give ground step by step in the initial stages. As the day wore on and the mist rose, we were able to see the hostile infantry advancing in masses, but they were paying a heavy toll at the hands of our machine gunners, who cut many a line in their ranks.

The (p. 063) situation became tense when the enemy succeeded in driving our men across the Bapaume-Cambrai road, and were seen to be approaching Anneux and Graincourt. The 18 prs. batteries which were lying alongside of us dragged their guns out of their pits on to the crest in front, and proceeded to rake the enemy, firing as rapidly as they were able, through open sights, the gunners stripped to the waist, toiling and sweating in their endeavour to stop the oncoming tide. The fight swayed backward and forward throughout the whole day, but finally the enemy was held in check without gaining further ground, and he incurred very heavy casualties.

In the south the situation was very obscure, and somehow or other the enemy broke a gap in the defences between La Vacquerie and Gouzeaucourt, capturing the latter place as well as the village of Gonnelieu, and commenced streaming through. He had advanced a considerable distance before the importance of his move was fully realised, consequently most extraordinary incidents occurred, stories of which are now familiar to everyone. Battery positions were rapidly overrun, and even wagon lines were captured, while Labour companies, working on the roads far behind the front, on looking up, discovered the foe almost on top of them.

There were no reserves in immediate support, and affairs were taking on a most serious complexion. Something had to be done and that right speedily! Therefore the Guards, who had only two days previously been withdrawn from the fight, were again called upon. They were lying in rest around Bertincourt, Ytres and Ruyaulcourt, and were hurriedly conveyed in 'buses and motor lorries to Metz, where they formed up and set out on their big counter-attack, supported by our sister Brigade and another gunner unit which chanced to have been pulled out on the previous night. Now, the enemy troops appeared to be as much surprised at their success as we were, and continued advancing in a bewildered kind of fashion, astonished at the little or entire lack of opposition with which they met. Suddenly, however, they came face to face with the full strength of the best disciplined troops in the world, whereupon they paused, staggered, and at length commenced to fall back, in confusion and disorder, with the result that the day was saved just in the nick of time, and most of the ground was recovered, in addition to some 50 guns.

Meanwhile (p. 064) the wagon lines were situated in the village of Ribecourt, right inside the salient, and, although it was known that a scrap was taking place, no one had any idea as to its stupendous nature. The fact that the village lay in a valley, surrounded by hills, prevented much noise of the conflict reaching those in it. However, shortly after breakfast, it became apparent that something was amiss, and the place became subjected to a heavy bombardment. The horses and vehicles were evacuated as quickly as possible, without suffering undue casualties, and collected on the hillside a short distance away, facing Bourlon Wood, where they "stood to" awaiting further orders.

Hostile aeroplanes put in an appearance, flying daringly low hither and thither across the salient, endeavouring to pick up as much information as possible, and sometimes dropping bombs. Many a tussle took place between them and our airmen, who did not allow them undisputed sway for long.

At noon instructions came through to be prepared to withdraw the guns at any moment, but in the end this was found unnecessary. Even at this time we were unaware that the enemy had penetrated our line to the south, and the first indication we had that something unusual was taking place, was the arrival of some reinforcements, who hurried along the top of the hillside behind us, and took up positions facing in the opposite direction! A short time elapsed, and then we were astonished and horrified to see a creeping barrage roll along, top the crest, and gradually draw nearer us from the rear. Fortunately, it stopped before actually reaching us, for by this time the enemy had attained his furthest point of penetration, and the counter attack had already been launched. Throughout the rest of the day the wagon line "stood to" ready for any emergency, and at dusk the limbers were sent up to the position, and the guns were withdrawn the same night and placed in action in the railway cutting immediately behind the ridge to the south of Flesquieres.

It became evident, after the experiences of the previous day, that, as long as we remained in this awkward salient, we would undoubtedly be exposed to further attacks at the hands of the enemy. The Germans meanwhile had concentrated huge forces in the vicinity, so a continuation of our advance was now out of the question, and a modification of our front was (p. 065) decided upon. The infantry constructed a new line running north of Flesquieres Ridge, and, as soon as it was completed, our troops fell back on it under cover of darkness, unperceived and therefore unmolested by the enemy, who only made the discovery on the following day, and then cautiously followed up until they came in contact with us once more. The salient presented a curious aspect at night to those inside it, and we seemed to be almost surrounded by Verey lights, as indeed we were, except where the narrow neck led out towards Metz.

The enemy did not, as was expected, attempt any further operations on a large scale, but contented himself with making things very uncomfortable for us. In spite of our withdrawal, the line was still saggy to a large extent, and he could bring his guns to bear on any part of the salient and enfilade it. He also paid much attention to bombing, and his planes came over at dawn and dusk and caused a good deal of damage. The wagon lines came in for their share of unpleasantness, and in the course of a fortnight we were forced to quit no less than three positions in turn. The battery was specially handicapped by the colour of its horses, and was evidently easily spotted by hostile aircraft, for we had more than our share of ill fortune at this period. To take the worst case that befell us, one night the wagon line lost 35 horses. A covey of enemy planes had been over at daybreak, and apparently made a mental note of our location, as they returned the same evening and dropped several bombs, though, strange to say, no damage was effected. However, towards midnight, a 4.2 battery suddenly opened fire with instantaneous fuse action, and many casualties were inflicted before the horses could be removed, owing to difficulties in the pitch darkness.

The most wonderful fact in the whole proceedings was that, although there was little or no cover for the men, who were ensconced in bivouacs, except a few who were in an old disused trench close by, only a couple of them were hit. The officers were rudely awakened by large splinters entering their tent, and only just missing their heads as they lay on their valises, while the sergeants had a most miraculous escape. They had formed a Mess in a bay of the trench, the sides supported and heightened by some of the Q.M.S.'s stores, and covered on top by a large tarpaulin. A shell dropped practically on top (p. 066) of them, fortunately detonating instantly against several boxes of iron rations, which undoubtedly contributed to saving their lives. An officer arrived on the scene immediately afterwards, and found them all lying unconscious as the result of the explosion, but they soon revived and took a stout part in rescuing the horses. The construction was completely wrecked, and the clothes they wore were stripped into ribbons, but only one of them had a scratch on him.

No delay was made in attending to the wounded horses, and in conveying the remainder to a place of safety. The drivers were all splendidly cool and collected under the trying circumstances, but many of the poor beasts were beyond human aid, and had to be destroyed.

The scene next morning was a gruesome one, and it was a most pathetic sight to watch the drivers, with tears running down their cheeks, bidding a last farewell to their lost charges before burial, for the men become exceedingly attached to their four-legged comrades, especially when they have had charge of them for a considerable time. No time was lost in selecting a new locality, as it was considered wise to get out of the salient altogether, and thus avoid the risk of incurring further unnecessary casualties; so the wagon lines were removed to the vicinity of Ruyaulcourt.

A spell of hard frost set in, with an occasional fall of snow, which added to our difficulties as well as to our discomforts, for it must be remembered that both battery position and wagon line were occupied at a moment's notice, and no time could be spent in making any preparations beforehand for our reception. Affairs were now settling down for the winter, and nothing unusual was taking place beyond a good deal of artillery activity on both sides, consequently we were only awaiting orders to withdraw from the line. These came through in a few days' time, and the Brigade pulled out in the middle of December to the ruined village of Beaulencourt, situated south east of Bapaume. On the following day a long march was undertaken, and we proceeded by way of Achiet-le-Grand, Ayette, and Beaumetz to the village of Montennescourt, due west of Arras, a distance of 25 miles.

It says much for the battery that it accomplished this long trail with no less than 43 horses below establishment, and without any outside assistance, in spite of the heaviness of the roads. (p. 067) The guns were pulled by six-horse teams, and the vehicles and other baggage wagons by four-horse teams, made up by requisitioning all the available outriders, yet none of the horses suffered to any great extent from the extra strain imposed on them.

It was with feelings of great gratification that we learnt that at last we were going to have our long-delayed rest, and that it would fall to our lot to spend the coming Christmas-tide and New Year season in more congenial surroundings than had been the case in the two previous years. All were prepared to enjoy themselves on this occasion, as it was felt, on reviewing the past six months, during which time we had been fighting incessantly in "pukka" battles, in which we had acquitted ourselves not badly, that we had thoroughly earned a week or two of complete rest and quiet.

# CHAPTER IX. (p. 068)

## At Arras.

The next fortnight was spent under most happy conditions, and all ranks had an enjoyable time. As Christmas approached, active preparations were made to excel anything we had ever had before in the way of festivities, and this was possible now that we were out of action. Quarter-Master-Sergeants, puffed out with importance, were to be seen strutting hither and thither, returning with mysterious sacks and parcels, presumably filled with good cheer.

Plucked geese and turkeys appeared in large numbers, suspended from the ceilings of billets, and several large barrels arrived on the scene, and were duly placed under lock and key in the canteen, awaiting the auspicious day. Much competition took place between batteries for the possession of the only two live pigs in the village, which eventually went to the highest bidders, while the remainder procured their joints in the form of pork from Doullens. One of the batteries meanwhile grew so attached to its prospective Christmas fare that it was almost decided to spare his life and adopt him as a mascot. His fate was sealed, however, when one day it was discovered that he had disposed of several parcels of food which had, inadvertently, been placed within his reach by some of the men.

Concerts were arranged, and the village school-room was kindly lent and artistically decorated for these occasions. The weather was all that could be desired now that we were safely lodged in billets, and it was a typical old-fashioned yule-tide, with a plentiful fall of snow followed by hard frost. The little village was in a sheltered hollow, and a small rivulet passed through it on its way down the valley, while the scenery might have been that surrounding any hamlet in the south of England.

An open air service was conducted by the Padre, for the Brigade, on 'Xmas morning, and the rest of the day was given over to sports and concerts, and the climax of enjoyment was reached (p. 069) at night when the men partook of their dinner. Gramaphones were well to the fore, but all kinds of musical instruments took part in the gaiety which followed.

A certain amount of latitude was given the men for a few days after, in order that they might recover from the orgy, for indeed they had never had such a gorge since their arrival in France. All were in excellent spirits, and these were by no means diminished when it became known that our next area was in front of Arras. It was recognised to be an enviable part of the line to be situated in, especially during the winter months. It was also a locality with which we had not as yet made acquaintance, and it was always interesting to visit a new portion of the front, as we disliked being too long in the same surroundings without a change of scene.

The day following New Year, the Division entered on its period of duty in the sector north of Monchy to the vicinity of Gavrelle, with the heights of Vimy, which had fallen into our hands in the previous spring on its left.

The battery position was reached by following the Arras-Plouvain road along the valley of the river Scarpe, and we took over from a Scottish Division. The enemy lines were everywhere overlooked, consequently he wisely refrained from showing much activity.

A magnificent view was obtained from the rear O.P. on the heights facing Vitry, and, on a clear day, Douai was plainly visible and even the country far beyond it.

Our front line ran along at the bottom of the slope, having the ruined piles of Roeux, which was the scene of such furious fighting in the latter stages of Arras battle, immediately in its rear. Half right, to the south of the river Scarpe, what remained of the village of Monchy stood out like a sentinel on the top of the hill. This point afforded a splendid view in all directions and was the veritable keystone of the whole position. Four of our pieces were placed in a quarry, a few yards off the road leading through Fampoux, on its western extremity, while the other two guns were moved forward, east of the same village, behind a bank, and carefully camouflaged. As this sector was extraordinarily quiet and there was not sufficient work to keep everyone occupied, the Battery Commander decided to commence construction and endeavour to make our position a model one. Two pits, which were already in existence, were pulled down and rebuilt, (p. 070) and two others were constructed alongside, and all of them were placed just as near the front bank of the quarry as would permit of the guns clearing the crest. The whole position was completely camouflaged, as, it will be readily understood, a quarry made a conspicuous target for the enemy at any time, and if he suspected the presence of a battery therein, there would have been little peace or quiet for us. However, as things turned out, we had evidently made a good job of our work, and to our surprise, not a single shell dropped in the quarry during our period of occupation.

Walls were white-washed and ammunition and charge shelves elaborately painted, the platforms were neatly tiled or bricked with material taken from the surrounding ruins, and all manner of "eye wash" was employed in making the pits look well. A communication trench was dug from one extremity to the other, rivetted and duck-boarded throughout, and led to the men's quarters. These when completed were palatial, and put in the shade any headquarter unit in the line.

The near side of the quarry, which consisted of chalk, was easily and rapidly mined, and, in the course of three weeks, the men had comfortable quarters. Beds made of wire netting stretched on wooden frames, a spacious dining hall, telephone pit, cook house, and they even possessed a moderate sized bath room, which was highly valued and put to great use. The officers' quarters were no less sumptuously fitted out. Each had sleeping accommodation, in cellars of the ruined houses, running along the main street close to the quarry, nicely lined with wood and canvas to keep the damp out, while the Mess itself was a work of art.

The latter was built entirely by the officers and their batmen, under the personal supervision of our energetic B.C.

The floors, walls and roof of the cellar were lined with three inch timber, and one day a subaltern, who had been out exploring, came back triumphant, bearing in his arms a huge roll of wall paper found buried under some rubbish, at a spot which probably denoted the one time existence of a decorator's shop. The Mess was therefore duly papered, with frieze complete, and with the addition of easy chairs, book shelves, a stove and gramaphone, there was nothing left to wish for, and the place was most cosy and snug. The entrance, too, was the admiration of everybody, nicely tiled and decorated with fancy carvings from the utterly destroyed (p. 071) church. Iron girders, beams, and countless bricks to the height of several feet rested on top of our home. It is not to be wondered at, then, that this model position was frequently visited by high personages, brought hither by our Brigade-Commander or C.R.A., who appeared almost as proud of the place as we were ourselves. Moreover, as we were in such close proximity to the road leading up to the front line, it was only natural that officers should drop in to this half way house and rest and regale themselves before resuming their journey, so before long our Mess was known as "The Pub" throughout the Division.

The forward position was treated in the same fashion, and never before had both officers and men had such comfortable quarters. Thus we settled down to a life of ease, such as we had not known since the Laventie days of two winters ago, and proceeded to thoroughly enjoy ourselves.

Frequent trips were made into Arras, either on horseback or by river, for there was a steamboat service, running daily on the Scarpe, which landed one close to the Officers' Club, a large wooden erection similar to a Y.M.C.A. hut, run by the Expeditionary Force Canteen.

The town had not been irreparably destroyed, and in most parts the inhabitants had returned, and were carrying on their usual routine, while many shops were re-opened and doing good business. The Cathedral was badly damaged, as well as other prominent buildings, but, on the whole, the town had escaped wonderfully considering how close the enemy had been to it for so long. Now, of course, the enemy was over six miles away, and the city could not be reached by any other than his high velocity guns, and they seldom troubled to shell the place, and when they did so, from time to time, the fire was chiefly directed on the railway station and sidings in the vicinity.

An equally peaceful time fell to the lot of those who were at the wagon lines. They were situated just off the main Arras-Souchez road, within easy reach of the former place. Accommodation for Officers and men was provided by Nissen huts, containing stoves, while the horses had good covered-in standings, with mud walls surrounding them for protection against bombing raids.

The transport of ammunition to the guns was easily conducted, as excellent roads ran the whole way, and every care was taken to (p. 072) keep the horses up to condition. The frost did not continue and in the early months of the year the weather was wonderfully bright and mild, and many a good gallop could be had in the neighbourhood, as there was a fine stretch of open ground close to the wagon line.

The horses undoubtedly had a better time than it is usually possible to give them during the winter months. The war horse is an extraordinarily intelligent animal and appreciates anything done for him in the way of comfort. He also becomes very cute and cunning, and always knows the routine of the day, and can tell his time of feeding almost to the minute, and, if allowed, would go by himself automatically to the water troughs and return to his own particular standing in the stable.

One horse familiarly known by the name of "Shrapnel," owing to several wounds of that kind which refused to close up, and completely heal, knew at once when he was "warned" for the line. Now, he disliked going out at nights, and consequently was in the habit of "scrimp-shanking," and proceeded forthwith to go lame. At first he managed to fool everybody, but on close investigation it was discovered that nothing at all was the matter with him.

Another fine beast, which at one time must have been ill-treated, when he came to us had a bad rope gall on his near hind, and was extremely nervous at being touched. After hours of coaxing he allowed his section officer and driver to handle him, and, at length, showed great affection to them both, but woe betide any other member of the battery, who attempted to go near him, back went his ears and out went his feet at once!

About the middle of February, a feeling of uneasiness evidently entered the minds of those in authority. It was known that the enemy was transferring large numbers of troops, which had been released by the collapse of Russia, to the Western front. Consequently every unit got busy at once, the Infantry dug new trench systems in rear of their existing ones, constructed strong points, and mile upon mile of barbed wire was laid down.

The gunners prepared new battle and reinforcing positions, in case a retiral should be necessary, and filled them with ammunition against all eventualities.

In a little more than a month everything was completed, and during the third week of March, the troops were warned of an impending great enemy offensive, and became fully on the alert.

# CHAPTER X. (p. 073)

**March the 21st.**

The morning of the 20th broke calm and the enemy did nothing to indicate that anything out of the ordinary was about to take place, but this did not deceive us, as it was known to our Command that the blow was going to fall on the following morning. Silence reigned supreme, except for the ordinary harassing artillery fire, up till midnight, but shortly afterwards the German guns opened out their annihilating fire, and drenched our forward system and battery positions with a severe gas bombardment.

In this area the majority of batteries had, at the last moment, taken the precaution to change their positions, as these were known to the enemy, and thus avoided being entirely demolished by the heavy concentration which poured all manner of shell into those they had lately vacated.

At dawn, which, unfortunately for us, broke in a thick mist, after a sustained bombardment of some four to five hours' duration, the enemy launched his gigantic attack over an area of fifty miles, from Guenappe, immediately below Monchy in the North, to the neighbourhood of La Fere in the south. Under cover of the mist, he congregated large numbers of field guns, which were able to accompany and closely support the attacking waves, while at some places he employed his new Tanks. These, however, though rendering some assistance to him, by no means came up to expectations, and were ponderous and clumsy, in spite of the fact that he had previously captured several of ours from which to copy, but they proved to be far behind ours, both in construction and usefulness.

A "Chinese barrage" was put down by the enemy on our sector, but no attack developed. The same evening the Division was hurriedly withdrawn from the line, and heading in a southern direction arrived in the neighbourhood of Tilloy and prepared for instant action.

In (p. 074) spite of the favourable conditions, our foes made little or no ground, throughout the day, on the whole of the Army front, and were held in our forefield. Further south, much the same thing happened, although they penetrated further in some places, but nowhere had they broken through, so the news on the whole was good and reassuring.

The German attack was renewed on the following day, and still the Northern Army remained firm, but they succeeded in effecting a serious breech in the Army to the south, where the British had lately taken over from our French allies. So swift was the enemy's progress at this point that our troops on either side of this bulge soon became endangered, and a general retirement was immediately necessary in order to keep the line straight.

This applied to the Northern Army also, but not to anything like the same extent. The Division again moved south, and took up positions behind the Henin Ridge, between the village of that name and St. Leger, for the purpose of covering the retirement.

The whole line thus became mobile, and, for several days, a stiff rear-guard action was fought, which resulted in very heavy casualties being inflicted on the enemy. He was by this time flushed with his success further south, and attempted to advance as if he were already the conqueror, which led to his own undoing, as virtually he was only permitted to gain ground at our time and will. It cannot be denied, however, that the days were anxious ones and the infantry were kept very heavily engaged and became much exhausted. However, they made the most of their opportunities, and had hitherto rarely found such ready targets, and their machine guns effected great execution on the enemy ranks as the men came along laden with full packs. A story is told, and is believed to be true, of one machine gunner that, in the course of his morning's work, he slaughtered over 200 German's single handed with his weapon, after which he became a raving lunatic and had to be forceably removed.

The infantry, too, admitted that they were getting tired of killing Boches, and the casualties inflicted on our men were a mere nothing as compared with those suffered by our foes. The gunners were equally busy dropping into action here and there and falling back as the circumstances required, until at the end of a week, the line became more or less stationary. The (p. 075) front line now ran through Mercatel, Boisleux and Moyenneville and thence, in a south westerly direction, towards Serre. Thus the Germans were again almost back on the line they had held, prior to the big retreat on the Hindenburg line in the spring of 1917.

It seemed a great pity to vacate the Henin Ridge, for the opposing sides found themselves facing each other in a hollow, with rising ground on either side, which made battery positions difficult to conceal. So many disused trenches, which had previously formed part of the old German line system, helped to shelter us, to a great extent, for we were at this point nearly two miles east of the permanent line of a year ago.

Everyone feverishly sat about digging and constructing new trenches, and an enormous amount of work was accomplished in a comparatively short space of time, for it was felt that the enemy had by no means expended all his strength, and would endeavour, in the near future, to resume active operations. There could be no doubt that he would be dissatisfied to remain where he was, especially as, so far, he had little to shew on this particular part of the front for his gigantic effort and huge loss of men.

It was no surprise therefore when, at the beginning of the second week in April, after a short sharp bombardment, the enemy made a strong attack from Monchy, north to the Vimy Ridge, with the object of seizing Arras and the heights before mentioned. The result was a costly failure, as he was everywhere held up in our forefield system, and the British Divisions opposed to him had the time of their lives. We were very interested to hear about this battle, as, of course, it was fought over the sector in which we had lately spent a number of happy months and where we had done such an amount of work. It was distinctly gratifying, too, when a wire was received from the Division who took over from us thanking our Division for the wonderful defensive construction made by us. It was due to that work that they were enabled to bring the enemy so quickly to an abrupt standstill.

They had seemingly experienced a veritable field day and thoroughly enjoyed themselves on that occasion.

After this unsuccessful effort, the enemy evidently gave up the attempt to gain possession of Arras and Vimy by a frontal attack and turned his thoughts elsewhere.

Unfortunately, (p. 076) however, in the course of these operations, Monchy had to be evacuated by the British, which enabled the Boche to gain observation on the city which, thereafter, came in for a good amount of shelling, and again the inhabitants were forced much against their will to leave the stricken place.

All manner of heavy shell fell in the town, and the damage caused was considerable, and it was no longer the haven of rest for the troops which it had been a few months previously. Our wagon lines, meanwhile, had not escaped undamaged, and were forced to change positions on several occasions until, at last, comfortable quarters were obtained in the little village of Bretencourt, where the houses still had roofs covering them, as the hamlet was just outside the devastated area. When affairs settled down once more, the battery positions were gradually advanced, and we dug a new position east of Ficheux, where the guns were meanwhile situated.

A forward section was established ahead in the railway cutting of the Arras-Albert line, and we subjected the enemy to as much unpleasantness as it lay in our power to devise.

We were not, however, any length of time in this sector, and were removed to the adjoining one immediately to the south.

The line required rectifying in several places, and in a brilliant minor operation, the village of Ayette was carried and remained firmly in our hands.

Our new position was situated on the high ground to the north of Adinfer Wood, immediately behind the village of the same name, but the neighbourhood was much more peaceful than that which we had recently quitted, as everywhere we had observation over the enemy, and naturally he never created trouble under such circumstances.

The wagon lines were again moved, this time much further behind, to the small village of Gaudiempre, where one might have imagined one was completely out of the war area, it appeared so quiet.

The place was intact and all were ensconced in snug little billets, while the horses were well off also, as opportunities for grazing were afforded round about the neighbourhood.

Then the enemy's second great offensive opened on the Lys, and all eyes were turned in that direction, but everyone held the opinion that, sooner or later, he would be brought to a standstill, which proved to be the case.

In (p. 077) fact, throughout the whole of this trying period, the confidence among all ranks was extraordinary. No one had the feeling that we were going down and under, and it would have done the pessimists at home a world of good to have caught a glimpse of conditions out in France and of the cheery optimism that prevailed there. There was even disappointment, in some quarters, that the enemy had not attempted to attack us on this front, but he evidently thought discretion was the better part of valour, for the defences were, by this time, very strong, and it would have been strange if he had managed to penetrate to any depth.

About the middle of May, it was the will of those in authority to rest the Division a while, and although we were not in any urgent need of a rest, we were not disinclined for it, as the season of the year was favourable, and we pictured all manner of good times in store.

The Brigade, therefore, withdrew to the wagon lines, marched the following day to Humbercourt, the village appointed for our resting place.

# CHAPTER XI. (p. 078)

**The Turn of the Tide.**

It invariably happened, when the Brigade came out for a period of rest, that expectations of a real holiday were never fully realized, and although the time passed pleasantly enough and we were favoured with fine weather, all ranks were kept pretty busy. Many tactical schemes were practised, and we had always to hold ourselves in readiness to render assistance, at short notice, to the troops who were in the line, for our Command was taking no risks and had not entirely given up the possibility of a hostile attack on this area.

It must be admitted, however, that in the end everybody enjoyed rehearsing these schemes, and we would have been well acquainted with our duties had the emergency arisen. Our resentment, also, at being called upon to partake of violent exercise so early in the morning, completely disappeared after a while, the country looked so beautiful at dawn, and we usually returned in time for breakfast, with well-whetted appetites, after some three or four hours in the saddle.

Unfortunately, at this time, the scourge known as "Flanders Grippe," which had been prevalent throughout the Army, developed in our Brigade. For a considerable time this epidemic paralysed us, more or less, as about half our number was down with the disease at the same time. Although it passes after taking its three days' course, one is left very weak and groggy for some time, and several of the men were very seriously ill.

Inevitable inspections by Corps Commanders and minor officials passed off without incident, but, of course, much labour and "eyewash" was expended as is always the case on these occasions. The Divisional Horse Show, held towards the end of our rest, was undoubtedly the principal diversion of our time out, as each unit naturally did its utmost to outshine all others. The battery entered a gun team complete, consisting of six dapple-grey horses, and we succeeded in securing the second prize (p. 079) in the gunner's Derby. Curiously enough, the winners, our sister howitzer battery, won with five, out of six horses which had been shown, over two years previously at Zeggers Capelle, in Flanders, and who then carried off second prize in the competition with a team of blacks. H.R.H. The Duke of Connaught afterwards inspected the prize-winners, and evinced much interest on being told that ours was a complete battery of grey horses.

Paris leave opened for both officers and men as a consolation for home furlough being stopped, and many availed themselves of the opportunity of having a few days' enjoyment in the "Gay City."

In the first days of June the Division returned to the line and occupied the sector we had already been in prior to moving to Adinfer. The area had become very quiet with one or two exceptions, and the enemy did not subject our infantry to much shelling, and contented himself with occasionally annoying them with trench mortars. But if, at any time, he discovered the location of a battery position, that unit had a most unhappy time. Four of our guns were placed in the railway cutting, where we had previously had a forward section, and the remainder were again detached some distance away. Mine shafts, which were already in existence, were enlarged and the men had plenty cover on top of them.

Some little time afterwards certain indications pointed to the fact that the enemy contemplated business once more on this front, and as our guns were situated awkwardly where it would be impossible to withdraw them quickly, we were directed to construct a new position further behind. The work proceeded briskly, and, when completed, four of the pieces were withdrawn and placed there, the other two remaining in the railway embankment. The main position was a long way back, and the guns could only just reach the enemy support trenches, consequently they were only to be fired in case of a general S.O.S., and all the shoots were accomplished by the forward section. Much time was spent in making our new quarters shipshape, and the ground was well suited for mining, as it consisted principally of chalk, and eventually all ranks were comfortably installed in spacious underground quarters, although, at the moment, they were quite unnecessary, and many lay out in the open during the warm summer nights. The principal thing to do now was to make sure that the officers and men did not stagnate for lack (p.

080) of occupation and to find means to keep them hard and fit. Physical exercises were indulged in during the morning, and sports of all kinds were organised, both at the battery positions and at the wagon lines—the latter having taken up their quarters at the village of Baillemont.

A modified kind of base-ball, introduced by an energetic and enthusiastic Canadian subaltern, became very popular with the men, while the corps ran a polo-club of sorts for the officers. A fairly level patch of ground was selected which possessed a certain amount of grass, and the numerous shell holes were filled in and levelled off by fatigue parties, with the result that it became moderately good. The polo ponies, however, left something to be desired, and it was no uncommon sight to see a young officer appear mounted on a stalwart wheeler, the best he could do for himself from among the horses in his section. Possibly the explanation was that he had found a horse which he could suitably "rein in".

Meanwhile the enemy's third big offensive had come and gone and the British Commander-in-Chief's famous "back to the wall" order of the day to his armies. Still we waited, but nothing unusual happened; then in the middle of July the French were heavily attacked, and once more the clouds appeared on the horizon. There was great enthusiasm when it became known that our Allies had counter-attacked, and were driving the enemy out of the Marne pocket, and when the daily bulletins arrived there was always a scramble among the men to read them. Then the British stroke fell south of the river Somme at Villers Brettonneux, and excellent news, as to our progress, came through, which raised everyone's hopes to a high degree. Our artillery fire was increased daily, and affairs became more lively, while flying was in full swing and continued night and day. Both sides paid much attention to bombing, and our Airmen freely besprinkled enemy territory with their bombs by day, whereas the foe rarely attempted raids over our lines during daylight. However, after dusk, the air was filled with the planes, as the weather was particularly favourable, and the hum of the machines coming and going was incessant throughout the whole night. At times one could scarcely get any sleep for the continual drone they made, like the hum of gigantic bees around their hives. One thing certain was that we had almost complete control of the air and both out-numbered and out-witted the enemy to a marked (p. 081) extent. It was most unpleasant to hear the noise of the hostile planes drawing nearer, for one could not mistake the beat made by the German machines. The amount of bombing experienced by us was quite bad enough in all truth, but we used to smile when contemplating what our foes must be suffering at the hands of our Airmen, as truly it was ten times worse.

During this period the two counter offensives were progressing favourably in the south, and we suspected that something would be doing on our front before long, as the din of battle was creeping further north. It came as no surprise, therefore, when serious fighting commenced north of the Somme, and the enemy retreated from Serre and later withdrew in error from Ablainzevelle. As soon as he discovered his mistake he attempted to retake it, but, by that time, our men were firmly lodged there and could not be shifted from the village.

In the middle of August, to everyone's satisfaction, it became known that we were to be up and doing at no distant date, and preparations were immediately and silently set on foot. Throughout each night a continual stream of teams and wagons conveyed thousands of rounds of ammunition up the line to battery positions, and fresh dumps were placed in forward localities. New battle positions were constructed in advanced positions and stocked with shells, and we only awaited the order to occupy them. Instructions were issued to wagon lines that all surplus kit and stores were to be left behind, as a strenuous time was in store for us, and all ranks responded with a will to the hard work these preparations necessitated. Drivers were elated at the prospect of a change from their humdrum existence, and their enthusiasm knew no bounds. New reinforcing batteries appeared like mushrooms during the night, and lay safely ensconced in their appointed places in readiness for the coming fray, while the neighbourhood behind the lines bristled with activity and also with new arrivals. We believed that probably these preparations were being made in order to take the Henin Ridge in front, and no one imagined that the coming operations would consist of more than a local attack with a limited objective, as little or no information had been given to anyone. It is true that rumours were abroad, that our opponents were preparing to withdraw during the coming winter to their defences in the Hindenburg Line, which meant that we would be left most uncomfortably situated in the wilderness throughout that season. Little did we dream, (p. 082) however, that this was the commencement of a long series of hammer blows, lasting over several months, and employing millions of men, and destined to be the last and greatest battle the world has ever seen, ending with the complete demoralisation of the enemy's forces. The turn of the tide was at hand at last!

# CHAPTER XII. (p. 083)

## Through the Hindenburg Line.

Before the serious work ahead of us could be undertaken, it was necessary to shear off an awkward little bulge in the enemy's line, which included the ruined hamlet of Moyenneville. The corps on our right were to take part in an assault two days previous to the commencement of our own advance, so it was considered expedient to accomplish the above task at the same time. Consequently, during the big attack, delivered in the south on the 21st of August, which brought our troops level with the Arras-Albert railway line, our small side-show passed off successfully almost unnoticed. Desperate fighting had also taken place in the neighbourhood of Morlancourt, just north of the river Somme, in which the enemy troops had been driven back after stubborn resistance. They thereupon evacuated the town of Albert, as the place was getting too hot for them, and retired on positions to the east of it. Our guns were now moved into their battle positions, and on the eve of the attack everything was ready and in order. For once in a way the weather was favourable, and this augured well for the speedy advancement of the guns, which was essential for the success of the operations.

At dawn, therefore, on the 23rd inst., without any preliminary bombardment, but, preceded by a dense creeping barrage and supported by innumerable tanks, the infantry set out on their long journey  The men swept on, capturing the villages of Boyelles and Hamelincourt at an early hour, without meeting much opposition or suffering undue casualties. The day went well throughout and all objectives were taken, and by nightfall, the vast machinery in the rear commenced to move slowly forward. Batteries were advanced and supplied with ammunition, by their echelons, ready for the next bout, and wagon lines occupied the positions only just vacated by the guns. The attack was continued on the following morning, which necessitated the (p. 084) moving up of the guns once more, and the same thing continued day after day. The enemy was slowly and relentlessly pressed back without a pause or breathing space, and once this gigantic force was set in motion it was exceedingly difficult to stop it, as our opponents were soon to find out to their cost.

As the fight proceeded, our comrades on the left joined in, and gradually the battle spread further north, assuming huge dimensions, until it reached the river Scarpe. The enemy was caught napping before Monchy, and the Dominion forces in one bound everywhere overwhelmed their opponents, not only capturing the village but gaining ground to the extent of two miles beyond it. By this time, Croisilles and St. Leger had fallen into our hands, but the enemy made a most determined stand in front of Ecoust, and a very stiff tussle took place for several days before we eventually gained possession of it.

Some extraordinary incidents took place during the course of these operations. The long-hoped for open warfare was upon us at last, and the gunners' dream of galloping into action and firing with open sights at close range was an accomplished fact almost before we were aware of it. On one occasion, the whole Brigade, immediately at the close of executing a creeping barrage, limbered up, and topping the crest in front came face to face with the enemy, and dropped into action alongside our advancing infantry. The enemy machine gunners were lined up on a ridge some four hundred yards away, but on seeing us they decamped with all speed, probably believing us to be a regiment of cavalry. At any rate, if they had stood their ground and manned their guns, they would have assuredly wiped us off the face of the map almost before we could have opened fire on them. At the end of another day's work, our battery position was scarcely two hundred yards behind our front line, where the infantry had installed themselves.

The wagon lines were now well over late enemy territory, on the ground where his batteries had been situated, and the mess was almost beyond description. In some cases his positions were entirely obliterated, which spoke volumes for the accuracy of the fire of our heavies, directed by our gallant airmen, and if it had not been for the quantities of ammunition and dead horses littered around, it would have been impossible to have known that positions ever existed there. Mine shafts had been entirely closed up by the explosion of the great shells, (p. 085) and a conglomeration of huge craters marked their locality. There was no rest for anyone these days, and no men were called upon to perform more strenuous work than our little drivers, whose untiring and never failing energy was worthy of the highest praise and admiration: not only had they to care for their pair of horses, but were incessantly on the go twixt gun positions, dumps, and wagon lines under the most trying and difficult circumstances, and, at the same time, the latter were changing positions frequently. However, they never faltered or grumbled, and had always a cheery smile on their faces, even when they returned in the middle of the night dead beat. For days on end it was impossible to get out of one's clothes, and sleep was almost an unknown quantity: however, what did it matter as long as we continued to advance, and in spite of everything—this was a long way better than the monotonous routine of trench warfare. Everybody looked upon it in this light, and the excitement and never ending novelty of the experiences under which we were living, carried us on through thick and thin.

The corps on our left, meanwhile, had by a superhuman effort penetrated the great Drocourt-Queant switch of the Hindenburg line, and firmly maintained their grip on the ground to the east of it, and all counter attacks made by the enemy, to dislodge them, proved unavailing. The troops to the south had also effected good progress, and the ill-fated town of Bapaume had again changed hands and passed for the last time into the keeping of the Allies. Thus it came about that the enemy troops, in spite of their very determined resistance in the neighbourhood of Ecoust and Mory, found themselves in a most perilous position, as the Dominion forces were now well in their rear, and were carrying out a turning movement from a northerly direction. Therefore, they were forced to do something, without further delay, which resulted in a swift retirement on to the Hindenburg line some six miles to the rear.

It was a most interesting and instructive chase, and the enemy retreated so fast that it was with the greatest difficulty that we could keep up and maintain contact with him. The battery had reluctantly to abandon a captured German field gun which had been doing valiant work as the seventh gun for several days against its late owners, for we had neither time or the means (p. 086) to convey surplus equipment along with us. It was the kind of day that one reads about in "Field Artillery Training" or even endeavours to imitate while manœuvring out in rest, but for the first time we were doing it in reality. The battery dropped into action on innumerable occasions during the course of the day, and had only time to fire a few rounds before the enemy had decamped out of range. Then we would limber up with all speed, the teams waiting the orthodox two hundred yards in rear and to the flank, and gallop forward and take up a new position right out in the open, and help the enemy on his way with a few reminders that we were up and after him, and that he would do well to hurry.

By evening our foes had snugly entrenched themselves behind the great Hindenburg barrier, and we again came face to fare with this formidable obstacle. The line had, meanwhile, been kept in an excellent state of preservation, and it was quite out of the question to make a frontal attack on it without first cutting the belts of broad wire and treating the emplacements to a prolonged bombardment. Another formidable hindrance in our way and placed between us, moreover, was the famous Canal Du Nord, which was entirely dry in most places. It was a considerable breadth across, and could obviously not be bridged as long as the enemy kept watch over it from the opposite side, and it varied from forty to seventy feet in depth. Thus, for the time being, the line settled down stationary until this task could be accomplished, for it was not the intention of our Command that we should sit down for the winter before this great fortress, as our enemies wished and expected us to do.

Our opponents were too busily engaged removing their heavy pieces of Artillery back to a place of safety to subject us to a great amount of annoyance, and, as the weather remained good, the work of bringing our heavies up was accomplished quickly and effectively. The battery took up a position in our former front line facing Bourlon Wood, with the ruined village of Mouevres immediately ahead, while the forward section was placed in part of the Hindenburg line itself, south-east of Pronville. Wire cutting was undertaken and carried out by all field batteries, and the heavies pounded enemy emplacements and communication trenches in the rear.

Bombing by aircraft became intensive on both sides, and the enemy adopted new tactics by coming over after dark, and, (p. 087) waiting for the gun flashes, proceeded to drop bombs on the batteries. A fine spectacle was witnessed two nights in succession in the form of a super-Gotha bombing machine brought down in flames. Our small fighting planes were in the habit of flying at a high altitude, keeping watch over our lines and lying in wait for these monsters. As soon as one of them was picked out in the rays of a searchlight, others would concentrate at once on it, whereupon the archies immediately opened fire. Then far above a light would twinkle out several times, which was a sign for the anti-aircraft batteries to cease fire. Everything remained still for a while, the searchlights always focused on their prey, which endeavoured to dodge out of the brilliant light, but in vain, owing to its unwieldiness. Then suddenly from out of the darkness a little object shot alongside the giant plane and spat tracer bullets into it, whereupon it instantly caught fire, and slowly heeling over commenced its downward journey to destruction.

Fierce fighting continued to the south, and by a series of brilliant operations our troops had everywhere come in contact with the Hindenburg Line, and commenced pounding its defences for the further advance. At the beginning of the fourth week in September preparations were almost complete for the coming assault, which would require all the energy and fortitude we could display. The Division was side-slipped down to the neighbourhood of Havrincourt, as it was familiar ground to us, after our experiences in November and December of the previous year. The policy at this juncture was, as far as it could be carried out, to place Divisions in localities with which they had already become acquainted. Our battle position was situated on the outskirts of the small hamlet of Demicourt, and we were to cross the canal a few hours after zero by means of a ramp already prepared and carefully camouflaged at a point where it passed through our lines. If all went according to expectations we were to follow a line due east, and, passing to the north of Havrincourt, take up a position, already known to us, on the railway cutting south of Flesquieres, although as yet it was in enemy possession.

The great battle opened on the morning of the 27th inst., under excellent conditions, and it is now known to everyone how the crossing of the canal was effected by means of scaling ladders, and, in some instances, by the use of life-belts.

From (p. 088) first to last the day went smoothly and well, and by nightfall the great Hindenburg Line, upon which the enemy depended so much and in which he had such faith, was everywhere behind us, and we were through, at last, to open country beyond!

It only remained for the Allies' great Commander-in-Chief to deliver the final knock-out blow at his own time and discretion.

At this time the writer was reluctantly forced to leave the Battery on account of ill health, and was sent home, and it is a source of keen regret to him that on that account he missed the closing weeks of the great campaign.

It is now a matter of history how our Armies, after hot and incessant fighting, swept the enemy divisions out of France.

On Armistice Day, the Division was in possession of Maubeuge, and thus the Guards found themselves on territory which they had occupied in the early days of the War, prior to the retreat from Mons.

After three and a half years of strenuous warfare, the Battery is now lying at rest in Cologne, where it keeps its silent "Watch on the Rhine."

**THE END.**